BEYOND TROUT

A Flyfishing Guide

BARRY REYNOLDS
JOHN BERRYMAN

with a foreword by John Gierach

trails books

AN IMPRINT OF BOWER HOUSE

DENVER

Cover Designed by Bob Schram
Illustration by Jay Snellgrove
Photography by Barry Reynolds & John Berryman, except as noted

Library of Congress Cataloging-in-Publication Data
  Reynolds, Barry.
        Beyond trout : a flyfishing guide / Barry Reynolds & John Berryman; with a foreword by John Gierach
            p. cm.
        Includes indes.
        ISBN 978-1-55566-156-4 (pbk : alk. paper)
        1. Flyfishing.   I. Berryman, John.   II. Title.
    SH456.R47   1995
    799.1'1—dc20   95-25661
                                                         CIP

CONTENTS

FOREWORD

When I first got into it, flyfishing was pretty much synonymous with trout or—if you lived in a different part of the country or had lots of money—maybe salmon or steelhead. The salmonids were where it was at; if you fished for anything else, you were slumming. Sometime back in the 1960s Robert Traver said he considered any fish that wasn't a trout to be "some kind of lobster" (good to eat, maybe, but no fun to catch) and that pretty much summed it up.

But I'd grown up with bass, pike, and panfish in the Midwest (caught on what I came to think of as "non-fly tackle") and I could never quite bring myself to consider warmwater and cool-water fish to be beneath my dignity. So when I learned, at first through the writings of Dave Whitlock, that trout weren't the only fish you could catch with a fly rod, I was delighted. If nothing else, I've always been a tackle freak, so this was an excuse to get some new rods and reels and tie a bunch of new flies.

Actually, flyfishing for bass and other warmwater species goes back a long way. The first cork-bodied flies are usually credited to Ernest Peckinpaugh around the turn of the century, and that was a new development in an old, established sport. It's just that, fifteen or twenty years ago, it had sort of fallen out of fashion. But then the articles began to appear in the flyfishing magazines and it looked pretty good. It also looked like fun—just plain fun, that is—at a time when flyfishing for trout was at the height of its tweedy, scientific stage.

I remember a classic Whitlock slide show from back then. There were lots of photos of big, goggle-eyed flies and huge bass, but the shot I recall most vividly showed Dave perched on the swivel seat of a gaudy bass boat with a fly rod in one hand and a martini in the other, silver-haired and grinning. Afterward, an angling entomologist-type in the audience asked him what aquatic food organism his Eelworm streamer pattern was meant to imitate. He said, "A grape-flavored rubber worm."

That would have been early on in what Jack Ellis calls "the Whitlock Revolution" when, Ellis says, dignity, artistry, and class came to warmwater flyfishing. That's true enough I guess, but I also like to think that, although it may have gotten a little more sophisticated, this kind of fishing has never quite lost its good old homespun goofiness.

In fact, I think it was in a Dave Whitlock article that I first read about carp being caught (on purpose) on a fly, a clipped deer-hair mulberry, if I remember right. All in all, it was pretty refreshing then and it still is now.

You hear a lot about advances in flyfishing—usually so-called technical ones—but I think the most important change I've seen over the last twenty years or so is that your average fly caster—once a trout purist—will now happily fish for just about anything that swims, with the possible exception of turtles and bullfrogs.

(Actually, bullfrogs *will* take dry flies, but never mind.)

It's great. If nothing else, having eclectic tastes opens up a hell of a lot more water, and with the sport of flyfishing growing like it is, we *need* more water. But I can't say I fish for pike, bass, panfish, carp, and whatever to protect the environment or to relieve the pressure on trout streams. Nor do I fish for bluegills in the apologetic spirit of so many of the magazine articles that have been written about them: that is, because they're closer to home. Where I live, trout are closer. It's a half-hour drive to the bluegills, and it's more of a production, too, what with the belly boat and flippers and the half-mile hike from the truck to the pond.

If there's anything wrong with all the current interest in flyfishing for warmwater and cool-water fish it's that—unlike twenty years ago when no one much cared—today I don't dare say where that pond is. If things keep going the way they are (and this book is a good indication they will), it won't be long before I'll have to get paranoid about my favorite carp puddles, too.

John Gierach, 1995

PREFACE

When I started working with Barry Reynolds on our first book, *Pike on the Fly*, I felt pretty smug. I had cleverly managed to hook up (no pun intended) with a genuine pike guru. All I had to do, I thought, was gather information from him, transform it into bytes and bits and then into something resembling prose, a book would magically emerge, and I would toddle off to other projects.

I neglected to take two things into account. First, Barry is one helluva lot of fun to work with—a natural raconteur, a logical thinker, a serious, dedicated adult flyfisher who has somehow managed to retain the boundless enthusiasm of a barefoot boy armed with a stick, a length of line, and a bent pin. Second, over the course of hours of conversations (it is an odd fact that the creating of something that is intended to be read involves about as much talking as writing), I realized that we were just scratching the surface.

Barry had applied the common-sense, methodical, practical, and most of all *effective* approach that characterized his pike fishing tactics to almost every freshwater fish to which he ever cast a fly. By the time we were two chapters into our first book, we were talking about this one.

And with the completion of our second book, I hope that you will have as much fun reading it and, above all, *fishing* it, as Barry and I had writing it.

John Berryman

ACKNOWLEDGMENTS

There are many people who helped make this book possible, but a few deserve special mention. All the illustrations in this book came from the talented hand of Jay Snellgrove. John Barr, Brad Befus, and Doug Tucker-Eccher provided flies, photos, and friendship. Len Sanders and Darrel Sickmon donated flies for use in photos. Dr. Steve Flickinger at Colorado State University and the helpful people of the Colorado Division of Wildlife gave hours of their time and a wealth of information to us. Van Rollo helped with contacts and gave us support. Louie Swift and George Bricher provided field research opportunities that were invaluable to us. Thanks, too, to our editors, Scott and Julie Roederer of Spring Creek Press and our publisher, Barbara Mussil of Johnson Books.

On a more personal side, we'd like to thank the long-suffering Reynolds family: Susan, Christie, and Mike; Cactus Kelly's Rod'n Gun Club; Jill (who thinks that one of us is cute, and that the other one is funny); Mom; Miss Duffield and Liesel Duffield; Wally Bupp, and Linda Rein (for cerebral Super Glue).

INTRODUCTION

When my friend Dan Mills called one day and announced that he'd be in Denver for a few days on business and said that he thought he could sneak a day's flyfishing in, it didn't take long for me to get the hint. I quickly suggested that we take advantage of that free day and fish some fairly remote gravel pits for smallmouth bass. Just as quickly, Dan agreed.

We met at an exit on the Interstate and made our way to the pits. Although we'd gotten an early start, it was already hot, and the air was still. All in all, it wasn't the greatest smallmouth weather. We began casting clipped deer-hair poppers in the shallows, and we caught some small fish. But no one is ever happy with small fish when big fish are around.

I switched to a Clouser Minnow and probed the first drop-off. This produced several decent fish. But it continued to get hotter, and really big fish were not to be had. We decided to move over to another pond and try our luck with some crappie. There we located a corner with lots of downed timber and deep-water access nearby. Things looked good. We tied on small black marabou Clousers and began working our way around the corner. Just as we were about to give up, we began taking fish. We got strikes from crappie on nearly every cast, just as our weighted flies sank to the appropriate depth. The fish were fat and sassy and terrific sport on a three-weight rod. We caught and released about thirty crappies in two hours. All good things must come to an end, and we finally caught all the crappie or the school moved off, probably the latter.

Dan and I moved once more. We caught smallmouth again and an occasional bluegill. A few largemouth served to keep us interested. As we walked back to the car, I realized that Dan and I had had an eight-species day: smallmouth bass, largemouth bass, spotted bass, white crappie, black crappie, wipers (white bass/striped bass hybrids), bluegill, and for good measure, a tiger muskie. Warmwater flyfishing does have its pluses.

We had caught just about every warmwater species except one. And the one we missed out on is one of the best kept secrets in all of flyfishing. It's overlooked and underfished, and the mere mention of it brings sneers, dirty looks, and sometimes laughter from other flyfishers. Do you know what fish I'm talking about, the one that you can catch virtually everywhere, the one that will make your drag scream and your heart race? The fish that unless it weighs over twenty pounds, is hardly worth talking about?

That's right, the fish we hadn't caught was the carp. If sight fishing for big, tailing fish that burn line off at an incredible rate interests you at all, then flyfishing for carp will impress the hell out of you.

All was not lost for Dan and me. As we walked back to the car, I noticed loose schools of two or three carp working one end of the pond. The fish had moved up on small, weedy flats and were rooting around for insects and small crustaceans. Just as bonefish do, they were foraging nose down, their tails giving away their location. I ran to the car to grab some flies. Dan watched, utterly bewildered, as I rigged up for carp. When I told him what I was doing, he chuckled (most anglers do).

The carp turned out to be grass carp or white amur, a close relative of the common carp, that had been introduced in the pit to control weed growth. After spotting a group of three fish, I carefully placed my fly several feet ahead of the fish and allowed it to sink to the bottom. I began slowly stripping the fly back, and one of the fish moved toward it. When the fish's tail came up, signaling that it was about to take the fly, I paused and then set the hook. In the shallow water, the carp had nowhere to go. The water simply exploded as it headed for deeper water with amazing speed. In a matter of seconds, the carp had taken me deep into my backing. He tail-walked across the little pond, showing no signs of tiring. Dan wasn't laughing anymore. After ten minutes of stubborn tug of war, thirty-five inches and about twenty pounds of grass carp lay at my feet.

Pretty? Not in the eyes of most anglers. Pretty intense? Without a doubt.

I urged a skeptical Dan to give carp flyfishing a try. Initially reluctant, he grabbed my rod when I pointed to two more tailing fish. Now, Dan's a fine fly caster, but his first cast lined one of the fish, and the carp spooked. The fish must have been in a forgiving mood, because one of them turned around, coasted up to the fly, and inhaled it. Dan was laughing again—not at the thought of flyfishing for carp but from the sheer enjoyment of catching one on a fly rod. Dan's first carp, caught on a Snapping Shrimp bonefish fly, was bigger than the one I'd caught. Another convert.

The point I'd like to make here and in the rest of this book is that warmwater flyfishing presents many opportunities to cast to different species, often in a single day and often within the same body of water. Unfortunately, some flyfishers take themselves too seriously at times, believing that some fish aren't worth their time or effort. They couldn't be more wrong!

Just about anything that swims can be caught on a fly rod, and anything that swims is worth catching on a fly. Not only will you become a better flyfisher if you fish for species other than trout, you'll be having a lot more fun. That's the point of all this, right?

With that in mind, let's begin our journey beyond trout.

Barry Reynolds

ONE

A Brief Look at Lakes

The first look at an expanse of featureless, quiet water can be very intimidating to a flyfisher who has fished mainly in rivers and streams. Anglers who are masters at reading the subtleties of riffles, runs, and pools often feel that the mysteries of a lake are beyond them. I can understand their feelings, for stillwaters in all their complexity warrant a book of their own.

The fish discussed in this book live primarily in lakes and ponds, and this chapter is intended to give you the background to become a successful stillwater flyfisher. In it, I hope to make lakes less intimidating by telling you how I've learned to fish them effectively with fly tackle. This chapter is by no means an exhaustive treatment of the subject. As your skill level increases, you'll want to embark on the same sort of systematic study—on the water and in the pages of books and magazines—that helped you become successful in fishing moving waters.

Although it sounds contradictory, stillwaters are dynamic, and their dynamics are complex. Indeed, the fact that a new stream can be "read" with fair accuracy by an experienced angler on his or her first visit might suggest to you that lakes are significantly tougher to understand. There are, for instance, no immediately obvious lies. The forces of moving water and bottom structure that channel food into feeding lanes aren't always as apparent in lakes. Water temperatures, clarity, oxygen levels, and general habitat conditions that are comparatively stable in rivers can vary widely in a lake. And bottom contours so easily seen in streams are often hidden by depth, weed cover, or discolored water.

All this said, it's easier to get started than you might think, because for flyfishers an in-depth study of the subject is overkill. A really thorough treatment of stillwater would apply more to anglers using conventional tackle who want to catch fish during the entire year. To do so, they must know where the fish are at all times and be willing to present baits or lures to them wherever they are. This can mean fishing the shallows or working great depths. Fishing through the ice may be required, as might trolling with lead-core line or downriggers. The use of live bait may be necessary to catch fish at all times of the year.

Conventional tackle permits fishing in all of these situations, but we're flyfishers. We can't work great depths effectively, we don't use live bait, and we don't really troll. With our tackle, we have to find fish when they're in comparatively shallow water, and that factor alone serves to reduce the complexity of lake fishing for us enormously.

Let's begin our study of stillwater with a look at a lake and its structure, with an emphasis on where you'll find fish.

Reading a Lake

In attempting to understand stillwater flyfishing, the first step is to reduce the size of the problem, and for the flyfisher, that's relatively easy to do. Take a look at a lake. It's certain that it's pointless to flyfish in areas where it's too deep to reach fish with fly tackle, so extensive portions of most lakes are really not of interest.

So, instead of looking at a lake as a vast, confusing expanse of water, I want you to think of it as an extended length of shoreline. As you work along that shoreline, you can fish water from six inches deep to as deep as you like. (In my own case, it's rare that I fish more than ten or fifteen feet deep with fly tackle.)

The challenge is to find habitat suitable for the fish you're after. With your depth limitations in mind, it's time to consider the lake from the perspective of the fish you're pursuing. Steep, rocky areas may hold smallmouth bass, while muddy bays with lots of weed cover may be good places to check for northern and largemouth. I'll discuss suitable habitat for individual species in the chapters that follow, and I'll tell you when you can expect to find them in that habitat.

As you learn the requirements of the fish, you'll know what kind of habitat you want to fish. Instead of walking the entire shoreline looking for it, here's a rule that (nine times out of ten) will serve you well, particularly in natural lakes: the nature of the lake's underwater structure along the shoreline will be very much like the structure of the land adjacent to it. A steep, rocky shoreline will give way to steep, rocky structure underwater. A grassy meadow will become a weedy flat. A creek flowing into a lake will have a channel that extends for some distance under water. In a manmade lake, roadbeds, ditches, fence lines, timber, and boulder fields that are visible on the shore will all probably continue for some distance under the surface of the water.

Studying the structure and character of a lake by looking at its shoreline will give you, out of all the area of the lake, the places where fish might be located within your depth window.

If one is available, a good topographic map of the lake can be a great help. Knowing the topography of the lake bottom will help you find drop-offs, weedlines, and other features that provide cover as well as feeding and spawning areas for fish. Many maps are actually keyed to the needs of anglers, with comments like "good for walleyes, April through June" inscribed on them.

A map provides a general guide to a lake's habitat, giving you some initial places to cast a fly, but you should go on from there to discover your own hot spots. There's a Colorado lake for which beautiful maps can be purchased, all of them full of helpful information for the angler. But my favorite pike fishing spot isn't marked on any of those maps.

As you fish a new lake or study a map of it, you should look for cover and "fish highways." Old creek beds, drowned ponds, railroad beds, and areas of high structural relief provide both cover and areas that concentrate moving fish.

A map can also help you find moving water. Yes, stillwaters *can* have areas of moving water in them, and they're important to your fishing! Inlet streams, for instance, pump food and highly oxygenated water into lakes. In the spring, a small inlet can also bring warm water into the cool lake, and those inlet areas can come to life first. For some fish, a warm inlet provides a spawning ground weeks earlier than the main portion of the lake. In the summer, an inlet may be a source of cool water, leaving fish accessible to you that would otherwise be forced out of the shallows. At all times, inlets can serve as food pumps that bring insects and baitfish to waiting fish.

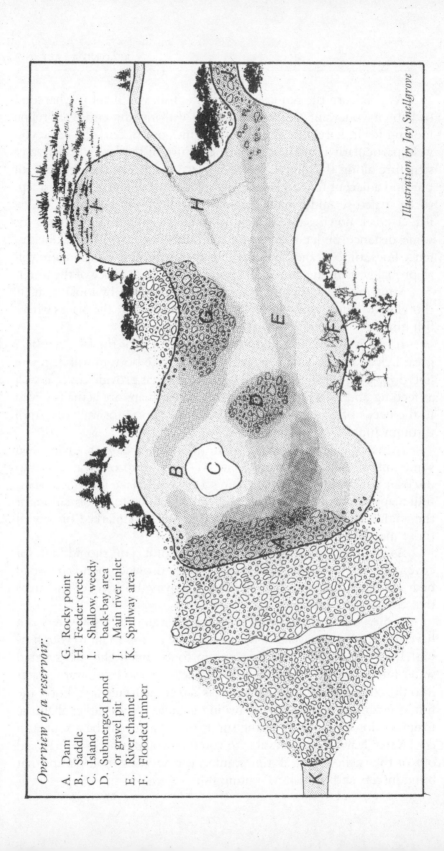

Overview of a reservoir:

A. Dam
B. Saddle
C. Island
D. Submerged pond or gravel pit
E. River channel
F. Flooded timber
G. Rocky point
H. Feeder creek
I. Shallow, weedy back-bay area
J. Main river inlet
K. Spillway area

Illustration by Jay Snellgrove

Outlets are also food channels, and fish will often stage at an outlet to take advantage of the insects and baitfish that are carried out of the lake. And finally, one lake's outlet may be another lake's inlet. This situation occurs when there's a small stream that flows from one lake to another. If the current isn't too fast, warmwater and cool-water fish may live in the stream, capitalizing on oxygenated water, food that's channeled to them, and stable temperatures.

A lake's inlets and outlets are obvious and more-or-less permanent—as long as water levels remain consistent, they'll continue to flow. But there are other areas of moving water within a lake that are more ephemeral.

Channels between islands and necked-down areas leading from one portion of the lake to another can, when sustained winds blow, become areas where currents exist. Fish locate on the "downstream" sides of these structures, both for shelter from the current and to prey on small fish and insects that are swept along by the moving water. Of course, as the wind direction and speed changes, so does the character of these temporary areas of moving water. What is the "downstream" side of a channel on Monday may be the "upstream" side by Wednesday—and by Friday, there may be no current at all.

While you're studying a lake, don't ignore other areas of mid-lake "shoreline." Islands have shorelines. Underwater humps and saddles between islands or between islands and the main shore can also have water within your depth window, particularly if the lake's water level fluctuates during the year. Because these areas offer fish rapid access to deep-water cover, they can be especially productive. A float tube or boat can get you to them.

All of these structural characteristics that we've been discussing so far are relatively fixed in character. Humps and channels don't move. Even the currents between islands or along channels can be depended on when the wind is blowing. But other factors that affect fish movement aren't as permanent and aren't visible, at least not on a map.

The Effect of Light

All fish are affected by light levels, and understanding the effects of light can be crucial when fishing for species, such as walleyes, that tend to hunt at night or prefer overall low light levels. One of the most universally accepted truths of fishing, particularly lake fishing, is that the best times to be out are early in the morning and late in the after-

Low light in early morning and late afternoon makes fish more active. John Barr

noon. The low light associated with those times of the day make fish more active.

Light does more than change at dawn and dusk, it also changes with the seasons and even during the day. In the spring and fall, you may experience a bright, sunny day, but remember that the sun doesn't rise as high in the sky as it does in mid-summer. The rays of the sun are hitting the water at a lower angle, more of the rays are reflected by the surface of the water, and the light level that the fish experience is consequently less.

During the day, clouds reduce light levels for the fish, as well. Less obviously, waves and chop also make it more difficult for sunlight to penetrate the water and can again permit fish to remain active.

Clouds reduce light levels, permitting fish to remain active.

Light and the heat that can be associated with it are the drivers for many of the dynamics of lakes. Heat (or its absence) is the compelling force behind turnover, an event we'll discuss later in this chapter. But light and heat are also the forces that bring the lake to life in the spring and, as they decrease in the fall, foster the yearly die-off in the shallows. The growth of vegetation, insects, crustaceans, amphibians, and mollusks and the feeding activity and spawning of fish are all dependent upon light and heat.

General awareness of the annual birth and death of a lake or pond is important, because it gives you an overall perspective of the forces operating on fish. As a lake is being "born" in the spring, fish move into the shallows to be part of (and to prey upon) the life that is burgeoning there. When a lake reaches "maturity" during the summer, fish leave the shallow nurseries to follow their prey as it moves into deeper water. And in the fall, when a lake begins to "die" and food becomes scarce, fish will often return to the shallows to hunt prey that has also come back to the shallows to feed. Finally, when the lake dies or, more appropriately, falls into a Rip Van Winkle-like sleep for the winter, fish also become less active and seek deeper water where they can await the rebirth of the lake the following spring.

The Effect of Wind

As we've already seen, wind can produce temporary currents in lakes and can also effectively reduce light levels under the water's surface. But wind can have other effects: it can affect local water temperatures, it can concentrate insects and other food, and it can affect water clarity. All these factors influence the movements and availability of fish.

Here's how wind can affect local water temperatures. The sun warms the surface of the water first. In the absence of wind, this results in a warm layer of water and, in the shallows, the creation of an incubator for plants, insects, and fish. If winds are present, they act primarily on the surface of the water, pushing the warm upper layer downwind. In the spring, when water temperatures are marginal, wind can make the shallows on the downwind side of the lake more productive.

The waves caused by wind also carry insects caught in the surface of the water, creating a concentration of food on the downwind side of a lake. Small fish are drawn to this food source and larger fish are drawn to the small fish. This effect of wind is often combined with discolored water, which I'll discuss in the next section, to provide just what big fish want: plenty of food and plenty of cover.

The next time you consider turning your back to the wind to make casting easier, think about the benefits of fishing the downwind side of the lake. The size and numbers of the fish there may make casting with the wind in your face worth it.

Transitory Cover

All fish like cover, and all sorts of lake structures provide cover for fish, most of it relatively permanent in character. But there are other types of cover that aren't as permanent as topographic structure and that are just as invisible on a map as light, heat, and wind.

One source of cover that changes with time is weed growth. In the early spring, a bay may be comparatively barren. As spring progresses into summer, weed growth often occurs. This has several effects. First, weeds provide shade that can make shallow water, which would otherwise be too warm, acceptable for fish. Second, the weeds provide food for insects and cover for baitfish, again making the area appealing for predatory fish. Finally, aquatic plants can increase oxygen levels in the immediate area, once again making it more appealing to fish.

There is such a thing as too much of a good thing. Weed growth can become so heavy that it is difficult for a large predator fish to navigate in and tough for you to fish, too. When this occurs, fishing the edges and gaps in the cover can be effective.

In the fall, the reverse situation can occur. The weeds begin to die off, and rotting vegetation reduces oxygen levels. The cover and food the weeds provided for insects and small fish vanishes, and predator fish must now forage in areas of more permanent cover or in deeper, still-living weed beds that are often beyond the reach of the flyfisher. Aquatic vegetation can be both a blessing and a curse for the flyfisher, and you should be aware of how weed growth changes over the course of the year in lakes you fish.

There is another source of cover and food that is even more changeable than weed growth—mud. On the downwind side of a lake, waves driven against the shore often produce a line between clear water and muddy water known as a mudline. Inlets, carrying unusually heavy water from a storm, can also bring mud into a lake. This "mud," stirred up by the waves or created by currents, is really composed of whatever loose stuff happens to be on the bottom. Some of it really is mud, but it also contains plants and insects that have been torn loose. Therefore, both food and cover are present for baitfish.

The mud also provides cover for cruising predator fish that can dart into the mud, grab a meal, and leave before the baitfish know what's happening. Areas of muddy or turbid waters are a favorite hunting ground for many of the fish discussed in the following chapters. The edges of stained waters are exceptionally good places to throw a fly.

Muddy waters are a favorite hunting ground of northern pike and other species.
Brad Befus

Rule-Breakers

Before I discuss when to go stillwater flyfishing, let's look at lakes that break the rules I've given you in the preceding pages. Most often, these are lakes formed as a result of man's activities. Quarry and strip mine ponds, livestock ponds, and small municipal ponds and reservoirs are all examples of these rule-breaking waters. In the case of quarry and strip mine ponds, the miners were more interested in extracting gravel or minerals than in making nice habitat for fish. Livestock ponds and small, primarily ornamental municipal ponds and reservoirs are often simply depressions carved out by a bulldozer. Once again, fish habitat wasn't a consideration. These sorts of impoundments often approximate the shape of a bowl; there simply is no structure, and in the case of a quarry or strip mine, the topography of the impoundment may bear *no* relation to the surrounding topography. What to do?

Here are a few things to keep in mind. First, you may think there's no cover in these manmade lakes, but fish are adaptable. In areas where cover or structure is lacking, even the smallest rock, hump, or depression may shelter fish. In such waters, fish may also seek out aquatic plants and use them in place of their preferred cover.

Often little is done to prevent erosion in these manmade impoundments. On the downwind side of the lake, prevailing winds may create shelves and overhangs that shelter fish. In other cases, erosion may cause banks to collapse, forming shallow areas that permit fish to spawn.

For some reason, after man digs a hole, he seems to have a deep, inner need to throw something in it. In many cases, the bottoms of these manmade lakes (particularly mining sites and quarries) are littered with old car bodies, scrapped mining equipment, discarded appliances, and building materials. Though not as picturesque as natural cover, it's still cover, and fish will use it as such. The trick is finding it. Because man is also lazy, he generally doesn't travel far to litter. The odds are good that most of the junk will have wound up reasonably close to an access road.

It also seems to be the case that when man digs a hole, he usually doesn't make it any larger than he has to. Most of these lakes and ponds will be small, and the smaller the impoundment, the more likely it will be relatively featureless. It may be possible for you to work the entire lake systematically.

And finally, if fish are present, they often didn't get there naturally—someone put them there. State and local recreational agencies usually make at least a passing effort to provide some sort of habitat for the fish they purchase with your tax dollars, and they often place

When waters begin to warm, fish move into the shallows. Charlie Meyers

brush, old Christmas trees, and artful arrangements of "found objects" in the water to provide cover. A call to the appropriate agency may provide you with some inside information.

Lake Methodology: When

Throughout this book, the "whens" will be based on water temperature. Fish move to areas of a lake where water temperatures are most comfortable for them. I use water temperatures to give you a general idea of what individual species are likely to be doing and where they might be doing it, but other factors, some of which I've already discussed, definitely affect fish behavior. I've focused on temperature in this book because it's the easiest part of the stillwater puzzle to solve—all it takes is a thermometer! That said, here are some qualifiers to keep in mind.

Understanding where fish reside in a lake at a particular time is tough at first. Although fish have preferred temperatures at which they like to live, they may have to leave them if food sources aren't present. Lack of cover in a preferred area can also cause fish to move to a more protected area, even if temperatures are less than ideal. Later, as you become more familiar with a lake, you'll be able to fine-tune your under-standing of fish movements by considering structure, local weather con-ditions, and what forage is available, along with water temperatures.

The different fish I'll discuss in this book exhibit the same very general sorts of movements over the course of a year. When ice comes off the lake and the waters begin to warm, fish move into the shallows. Once there, they generally feed heavily for a time, and they spawn (some species guarding the eggs and fry, others abandoning them). After the spawn, most species move into deeper water and sulk for a time, and then return to the shallows, which are bug and baby fish fac-tories, and again feed heavily. In some lakes, fish can remain in the shal-lows for months; in others, rising temperatures will drive them and their prey out into cooler, deeper water. The movement of fish in search of cool water means that flyfishing may not be productive at certain times of the day or at certain times of the year.

As fall arrives, the water cools again, permitting fish to return to the shallows, where they feed heavily to build up the fat reserves that will take them through the winter.

Yes, this is a very simple model, one that could be summarized as:

Into the shallows—as the water warms, to feed heavily and spawn
Out—after spawn for a brief rest of a week or so
In again—to resume feeding
Out again—when and if it becomes too warm or food sources leave
In—when it cools, to feed heavily
Out—to spend the winter in the depths

The model is so simple, in fact, that I must now shoot a few small holes in it. The model is a very general one that I'm presenting as a beginning step in understanding the movement of fish. Many factors affect the model. For example, a cold snap can bring spawning to a halt. Fluctuating water levels can interfere with the movements of fish. A warm fall, early spring, or excessively hot or cool summer can all change this rather ideal picture significantly.

Yes, you'll study stillwaters, and you will do so just as seriously as you now study streams. But with the above qualifiers in mind, this sim-ple model is a "back-of-the-bar-napkin" concept that will work for you. Twice a year, however, all models of fish behavior break down in most lakes. Let's take a look at the seasonal changes that affect the fishing.

Seasonal and Weather Changes

Until you begin to know a lake, it's easy to think of it as an expanse of unchanging water. Nothing could be further from the truth. The water in most lakes is in a constant state of change, often invisibly, and understanding these changes can help you find fish.

Since water temperature is one of the major factors in where fish will be found, I've spent a lot of time discussing it in this chapter, and I'll continue to do so in the chapters about each species. All fish have a preferred temperature range. Find water in that range, along with suitable habitat and food, and you'll likely find fish. That may sound relatively easy, but water temperatures change with the seasons and the weather, moving fish to different areas of the lake.

Perhaps the most dramatic changes happen in the spring and fall in all lakes, except those in the southernmost part of the country. Driven by changes in temperature, the water in lakes mixes. This phenomenon is known as turnover. The end result of turnover is an equalization of water temperatures and oxygen levels throughout the lake, destroying existing stratification and usually causing fish to scatter until the lake stratifies again. If you don't understand turnover, there will be at least two times in the year when everything you know about fishing in lakes will be thrown out of kilter. Fish won't be concentrated in the areas you're used to fishing, since the limitations of water temperature no longer restrict their movement.

The mechanism of turnover revolves around an odd characteristic of fresh water: at thirty-nine degrees Fahrenheit, water is at its densest. Warmer water will float on thirty-nine degree water, and so will water that is colder. As winter approaches and waters begin to cool, the surface of a lake cools first. Finally, it will reach thirty-nine degrees. This dense water sinks, and that drives warmer water to the surface, where it in turn cools, sinks, and drives more warm water to the surface.

The end result is that the lake mixes—turns over—and oxygen levels and temperatures throughout the lake equalize. This permits fish to scatter, and fishing can be tough until the lake begins to restratify.

Warming temperatures in spring present a similar scenario. Ice melts, and the surface waters reach thirty-nine degrees. This dense water sinks, driving less dense water to the surface where it in turn reaches thirty-nine degrees, sinks, and drives less dense water to the surface. Oxygen levels and temperatures equalize throughout the lake, and the fish disperse—again making fishing tough. As temperatures continue to warm, the lake restratifies, and fish return to their accustomed haunts.

Routine weather changes can also cause changes in water temperature and additional mixing of waters. Winds move water, sometimes creating the equivalent of currents and often changing the temperature of water in certain areas of a lake. All these factors impact where fish will be found.

Opinions abound concerning the effects that weather conditions have on fishing. Personally, I have seen pre- *and* post-front conditions both improve *and* degrade fishing. Based on personal observation, my feeling is that what fish want most from the weather is consistency and stability. However, as far as I'm concerned, making blanket statements on the effects that weather conditions may have on fishing is risky.

All of the forces, including seasons, weather, and wind, that induce changes in the "still" waters of a lake dramatically affect the fishing. For now, it's enough to understand how dramatically water moves and changes in lakes throughout the year.

Using the Book

Throughout this book, I'll give you general water temperature ranges that affect fish and determine their locations: when specific fish begin to move into the shallows, when and where they prefer to spawn, the general ranges of temperatures at which they prefer to live, and the upper and lower temperature limits that they can tolerate before they move into deeper water.

Those temperature ranges, coupled with local inquiries and your overall understanding of the character of the lake, are your guides to successful lake fishing.

For instance, in the spring, if the water temperature is in the low forties, you probably won't find me checking bass spawning areas, but you can bet I'll be in weedy, shallow areas preparing to knock over a few northern. If the water temperature is in the mid-forties and it's a bright, sunny day, I might leave my beloved northerns in mid-afternoon to get a crack at pre-spawn smallmouth moving in for an hour or so when the water temperature on a gravelly flat just might rise to the low fifties. In my area of the country, you probably won't catch me flyfishing for walleyes in June; they've gone deep and are out of reach. But largemouth are right where I want them—shallow and hungry.

Local inquiries play a prominent role in my gathering of information. In the past twenty years or so, a network of fly shops has sprung up across the United States. It's not at all unusual to go into a shop

With water temperatures in the low forties, I'll be in weedy, shallow areas looking for northern pike. Bryce Snellgrove

and see a blackboard with the flow rates, water temperatures, water clarity, current hatches, and effective imitations for local streams listed. In many fly shops, the dramatic rise in interest in fishing for bass, panfish, northern pike, and other "beyond-trout" species have resulted in similar information being displayed for local lakes and reservoirs.

It may also be time for you to make some new friends. Seek out new acquaintances in bass shops (they've multiplied like mad, too) and at meetings of bass, walleye, and muskie clubs. If you're a dyed-in-the-wool trout fisher, you'll probably be amazed to learn that people who fish for these species are just as crazy as trout anglers.

In Summary

Learning to fish lakes and learning to fish for new species requires study. My home lake is literally within sight of my house and has fine populations of tiger muskies, trout, perch, and bass. The lake is the recreational centerpiece for a Denver suburb, and although it is fished very heavily, my tippet-class world record tiger muskie (and the even larger Colorado state record tiger) came from its waters.

In the spring, just as the ice goes out, I'll fish weedy flats for tigers and trout. But I also keep an eye on the weather and on my thermometer.

As the waters warm, I can go to a shallow area of the lake and, in a few hours, catch twenty or so pre-spawn bass. They respond to the small window available to them when the waters warm just enough to permit foraging in the shallows. As the days grow warmer, they'll spend more time in those weedy shallows, finally spawning there. And the best part is that of the thousands of anglers who fish this lake, there are very few of them taking advantage of this bonanza—the others didn't do their homework!

I wrote this book to give you the basic information you need to allow you to be at the right place at the right time, to enable you to go "beyond trout" successfully. You're probably a pretty serious fly-fisher (or thinking hard about becoming one); otherwise you wouldn't have purchased this book. I hope you like flyfishing because you find it to be a great deal of fun. In my opinion, there is nothing that can make the sport less fun than being stubborn about it. While you can probably catch a walleye in July on a fly, I can also almost assure you that doing so will be a slow, boring process. Your time might be much better spent in pursuit of largemouth bass.

To help you target the times and places that are likely to be best for flyfishing, the upcoming chapters will cover when (in terms of temperature) and where (in terms of habitat) you might successfully fish for species such as northern pike, bass, sunfish, crappie, and walleye, among others.

Let me add a few warnings. First, fish are individuals. "Spawning temperature" means that, as a rule, most fish of a particular species will be in the spawning mode if the water is at that temperature. Some of the fish will be preparing to spawn, many will be in the act of spawning, and some will have already spawned.

Second, fish are confronted with the same imperfect world that we face. But they are also at least as adaptable as we are. The temperatures listed here are averages. Almost certainly, conditions where you live will change the circumstances presented in this book to some extent.

And third, I've been sneaky. To make very sure that you don't rely too heavily on the information presented here (as opposed to assembling your own), I've deliberately used fairly large temperature ranges throughout the book. Local conditions and the likes and dislikes of individual fish make any information in any book a general guide, not a message from on-high!

Now let's take a look at our first beyond-trout species, the ubiquitous sunfish.

TWO

SUNFISH

Many years ago, on farm ponds and lakes within bicycle-range of my home in Texas, I cut my flyfishing teeth on sunfish. The flashy little fellows took my awkwardly-cast fly often enough to keep my confidence up, and my early success kept me coming back for more. Bigger sunfish taught me the importance of stealth, of delicacy of presentation, and the importance of properly-tied knots and unfrayed tippets.

On light fly tackle, a day spent in pursuit of six- to eight-inch sunfish can be great fun, and sunfish are an ideal starting point in your journey "beyond trout." Sunnies take a fly willingly and aggressively. They are a fine fish upon which to build the fundamental skills that will enable you to tackle more challenging—but never gamer—species.

When there are sunfish are to be had, you're very likely to catch some. If you're a newcomer to flyfishing, small sunfish will accept the fumbling casts and noisy presentations that are part of the learning process. But big sunfish, the pound-plus, salad-plate-sized fish that have survived predation from virtually everything that swims, flies, wades, or boats, are just as clever, just as likely to refuse a poorly presented fly, and just as likely to flee from an awkwardly-cast line as are big, experienced bass or trout.

If sunfish weighed six pounds, no one would bother fishing for anything else. Brad Befus

Most of the sunfish you catch, at least at first, will be small, perhaps a half-pound, but on light tackle and tippets, they'll give you a fine tussle. The occasional three-quarter- to one-pound fish will astound you with its strength, and a two-pound fish in heavy cover is thrilling on trout-weight gear.

Recently, a friend and I had an opportunity to fish some private ponds that are home to some genuinely large sunfish—a one-pound fish is fairly common. But fish don't get big by being stupid, and in order to catch those old pros, my friend and I found ourselves sneaking around in crouched positions and casting as carefully and precisely as we would to rising browns. At the close of the day, my friend commented, "You know, if these things weighed six pounds, no one would bother fishing for anything else."

I think my friend was right.

Although I've referred to sunfish as our first stop and as a fish to learn on, the pursuit of trophy sunfish can become a passion just as consuming as the pursuit of any other trophy fish. Whether you're a beginner using sunfish as a learning fish or an experienced flyfisher stealthily searching out trophies, you'll learn much from them—and you'll have a ball in the process.

Sunfish Habits and Habitat

Sunfish are part of a large family of fish that includes bass and crappie. There are nearly two-dozen kinds of sunfish (genus *Lepomis*, if you care about such things) in the continental United States. In the South, incidentally, sunfish are called bream, a generic term that is always pronounced "brim" by real southerners.

Sunfish date back to at least the Cenozoic era, about sixty million years ago. Originally found only east of the Rockies, sunfish are now found everywhere in the continental United States. There are many species of sunfish, including longear, redbreast, and redear sunfishes, and many hybrids that occur in lakes that are home to more than one species. Due to their widespread availability, three species are likely to be of most interest to you: bluegill, pumpkinseed, and green sunfish.

There are significant differences between the species. The following chart should assist you in keeping these differences in mind. When I talk about pre-spawn, spawn, and post-spawn behavior, a quick referral to the chart will give you the approximate water temperatures, conditions, and preferred habitat for the three sunfish species covered here.

Bluegill

Habitat: Prefers some weedy cover; tolerates brackish water.
Preferred Food: Insects, crustaceans, minnows.
Spawning Temperature: 68°–72° F.
Nest Type and Water Depth: Sand, gravel, firm bottoms; 10″–30″.
Identification: Vivid turquoise slash on lower gill plate, orange/rust on throat; large fish to 10″/1 lb.

Pumpkinseed

Habitat: Smaller lakes, bays in larger lakes, ponds; prefers shallower water, heavy weed cover.
Preferred Food: Insects, also small crustaceans and minnows; small mouth limits prey size.
Spawning Temperature: 66°–68° F.
Nest Type and Water Depth: Sand, gravel, firm bottoms; 6″–24″.
Identification: Vivid shades of green, olive, rust, orange, and gold; small mouth and smaller average size (6″).

Green Sunfish

Habitat: Adapts better to turbid waters, low oxygen levels; prefers heavy cover.
Preferred Food: Comparatively large mouth permits fish to take larger prey, e.g., small crawdads and minnows.
Spawning Temperature: 68°–72° F.
Nest Type and Water Depth: Small rocks; 6″–18″.
Identification: Most "bassy" in appearance, large mouth, subdued coloration, rarely over 6″.

Bluegill Habits and Habitat

Day in, day out, the sunfish you're most likely to find yourself casting to is the bluegill, and (at the risk of violating many sensibilities) it's the bluegill that we will discuss in the balance of this chapter.

The bluegill (*Lepomis macrochirus*) lives in lakes across the Lower Forty-eight states and is characterized by a vivid turquoise splash of color across the lower portion of the gill plate and a rusty or orange chest. However, many different color variations exist, and depending on water clarity and chemistry, 'gills can range from a nearly translucent silver to extremely dark brownish-bronze.

Prolific spawners, bluegills can easily overpopulate a lake without adequate predation, resulting in large numbers of stunted fish. A healthy female bluegill can lay nearly 40,000 eggs, and because the males guard the nest, baby 'gills have a better chance at life than other fish. Spawning commences in the spring and can continue for months. In some areas, bluegills may spawn from spring to late summer.

Small bluegills feed heavily on insects and small crustaceans, such as scuds and freshwater shrimp, and can be found in the shallows during most of the day. Large bluegills prefer meatier stuff in the form of minnows, small crawdads, and leeches. They're more likely to be found in deeper water—but still often within the reach of fly tackle.

Although bluegills are very adaptable, as demonstrated by their wide distribution, they like clear water when they can get it. They can be found in ponds, lakes, reservoirs, and slowly-moving rivers. A one-pound bluegill (about a ten-inch fish, and likely to be in the neighborhood of ten years old) is bragging material, but the world record bluegill (caught in Ketona Lake, Alabama in 1950) was a monster that weighed over four-and-a-half pounds.

Bluegills feed most heavily during the morning and early evening hours. Night fishing on moonlit nights or near lights can also be productive. However, feeding activity is also a function of food availability,

Day in, day out, the sunfish you're most likely to cast a fly to is the bluegill.

particularly in lakes where sunfish have overpopulated. When there is an insect hatch during the middle of the day, small sunfish actively take emergers and rising nymphs, and large sunfish that come to prey on baitfish feeding on insects are not above grabbing a bug or two.

Bluegills also have, in the language of the technically inclined, a strong tendency to "relate" to objects or structure in their environment. What this means in the more prosaic language of the angler is that bluegills will generally be found near something. Many fish relate to structure, but bluegills seem to need to do so more than most. Bluegill will be found near a stump, the branches of a submerged tree, the pilings of a dock, nooks and crannies of a rocky bank, a large rock, a submerged hump or drop-off, a sunken tire, or an old car body. All of these things provide cover for the fish, but I've also seen bluegills congregate around buoys, moored boats, and swimming platforms where they're extremely exposed. This desire to relate, even at the expense of cover, can result in some interesting situations.

As noted earlier, *everything* eats sunfish. There have been many occasions when I've lobbed a little popper under a dock and hooked a nice 'gill. I'll settle down to enjoy a good scrap on light tackle when suddenly my little bluegill will vanish, swallowed by a much larger northern or largemouth. My light tippet usually won't take much of this sort of abuse, but for a few minutes, things can become very exciting!

Seasons of the Bluegill

Let's follow the bluegill through the year to identify the best times and places to fish for them. Remember that most of this applies to the other sunfish, as well, but keep in mind the differences in the preferred water temperatures and spawning habitat previously mentioned.

Pre-spawn Bluegills

Spring means pre-spawn fishing, and for bluegills, spring begins when water temperatures reach about sixty degrees. When the water warms to this temperature, bluegills move near spawning areas from the deep water where they've waited out the winter. Typically, this means that the fish will congregate close to nesting areas, in water that is a bit deeper than their spawning beds proper. If you're new to a particular lake, it may be worth your while to have a word with a local guide, marina operator, or someone who's been fishing the waters for some time, because all sunfish will seek out the same spawning areas from year to year, and the locals are likely to know where they are.

Staging areas can range from as shallow as two or three feet to as deep as eight or ten feet. For my money, fishing in ten feet of water with light fly tackle isn't much fun, so I elect to work shallower staging areas no deeper than four to six feet.

I also seek out bays with dark, firm bottoms. Most sunfish prefer to spawn in sandy or gravelly areas, and a darker bay will warm faster than the surrounding lake. As the water temperature increases to the mid-sixties, the bluegills will move to their spawning beds during the heat of the day and back out again when the water cools. When the water is consistently in the high sixties, the fish will remain on the beds and serious spawning activity will begin.

While bluegills like a gravelly bottom, they may not be able to get one. Don't ignore areas of emerging vegetation or established weed beds. Prime spawning areas will have some cover to which the fish can relate. This can mean natural cover, such as brush, submerged trees, stumps, or weeds, or man-made items, such as submerged tires or car bodies. In a little puddle of a lake in a housing development where I lived as a boy, pre-spawn sunfish liked to stooge around a submerged box spring that lay in about five feet of water. I can't tell you how many of my flies wound up tangled in its springs.

Feeder creeks, pumping warm water into the lake, can also be good locations to find pre-spawn bluegills. But beware of a swiftly rushing, muddy stream. These fast waters may not have had time to warm sufficiently, and bluegills simply don't like to spawn in the muddy sediments that such a creek will inject into the lake.

At this time of year, you should take into account the following factors. First, the bluegills are anxious to spawn. During the heat of the day, look for them to begin moving into the shallows. Preliminary nest building may commence at this time, and you may see some discolored water or muddy areas where the males have been working. Second, the shallows are coming to life along with the rest of the lake. Bluegills will take advantage of this by moving into the shallows to feed. Early in the season, before the fish are consistently in spawning areas, feeding opportunities will encourage a move to the shallows during the heat of the day, when temperatures there rise enough to stimulate feeding.

Spawning Bluegills

Like other members of their large family, bluegills are a nesting fish. The males set up housekeeping and use their tails and fins to dig a bowl-shaped nest perhaps two inches deep and as much as a foot in

Male bluegills set up housekeeping by digging a bowl-shaped nest two inches deep and a foot in diameter.

diameter. When favorable spawning areas are limited, sunfish can establish a regular housing development with nests literally within a foot or so of each other. To the saltwater angler, these clustered nests will be reminiscent of the pockmarked areas where bonefish have been working. Oddly, the flashy bluegill is beautifully camouflaged in the water, and I often find the nests much easier to spot than their guardians.

During mating, the female deposits her eggs in the nest and the male fertilizes them with his milt. The female then leaves the scene, staying in deeper waters during the heat of the day and moving into the shallows at dawn and dusk to feed. The male assumes the task of guarding the eggs (which hatch in about five days) and will even remain with the fry for several days after they've hatched. At this time, male bluegills are extremely aggressive, and it's possible to catch the same fish several times in succession. Obviously, it's important to get these fish back into the water quickly, so that the eggs and fry can be protected.

Aggressiveness of males at this time of year can approach the ludicrous. I've fished ponds where available spawning areas are limited, and the housing developments are crowded. The poor males are in a constant snit, alternating periods of glaring at their neighbors with frantic attacks on anything that comes too close to the nest. This can result in the males engaging in shoving matches when a fly appears between two nests—the fish literally fight for the honor of grabbing the fly!

The spawning season can last for some time—with stable temperatures, bluegills can spawn two or even three times a year. This results in cycles of activity that, in the best of all worlds, lasts all summer long. Groups of bluegills will spawn together several times, resulting in repeated periods of a week or so when the action becomes very hot.

During the spawning season, clever sunnie anglers routinely check spawning areas and adjacent staging areas as spring progresses into summer. Fishing in the nesting areas may taper off for a time (and that's when you should check out the staging areas), only to rebound when a new crop of fish are ripe.

During the spawn, catching bluegills (and the males in particular) will not be a problem. *Everything* that intrudes on the nesting area is attacked. This includes large fish like bass, and as I remember from my childhood, even the bare legs of a skinny, wading, twelve-year-old flyfishing wannabe.

There is another thing to remember at this time of the year. If you've found the nests but tire of catching eight-inch fish, move a bit deeper. Large sunfish tend to spawn deeper than their smaller brethren, and although the nests may not be as visible in the deeper water, large fish may be in the area—if the lake isn't overrun with stunted fish.

During the spawning season, your intent is to catch the attention of a fish that is either feeding heavily to support the spawn or in a combative mood because it's guarding the nest. It's a great time for surface action. Recently, much attention has been focused on using conventional dry flies and "hatch matching" for surface-feeding sunfish. Although I don't get very serious about matching the hatch, I use flies such as Humpies, Adams, and Irresistibles. Caterpillar, ant, and beetle imitations and a variety of free-form, rubber-legged horrors tied in sizes 12 to 16 round out my surface flies. I also do a lot of fishing with tiny poppers, size 14 to as small as size 18. These work fine for me, and they're lots of fun to use. In my experience, spawning sunnies seem to show a preference for yellow, chartreuse, red, black, and white corks.

A small Woolly Bugger (size 12 or 14) in white, black, olive, or a bright color for use in murky water is a good choice for subsurface work, particularly if you're trying to reach larger fish nesting in deep water. Streamers such as small Zonkers, any of the D's Minnow patterns, and any of the traditional streamer patterns are also good choices. The key word is small. Even a big sunfish may have trouble getting a grip on a size 8 streamer. If you feel hits but fail to hook up, go down in size. Nymph patterns are also worth a try. I like to use damselfly and dragonfly nymphs, because they're swimmers and I can retrieve them with some action. Day in, day out, however, I use a fat Hare's Ear Nymph in sizes 14 or 16 for most of my nymph fishing.

Post-spawn Bluegills

Post-spawn should really be considered pre-summer, and your tactics will be a function of the lakes you fish. As we've seen, in some lakes and reservoirs, spawning will continue for months, and there may be no post-spawn as such. In others, the fish may spawn only once and go into a true post-spawn pattern, marked by a move to deeper, cooler water.

The staging areas you fished early in the spring are good places to look for post-spawn fish, remembering that often the fish really are staging, in the sense that some fish may be preparing to spawn again, while others are waiting for preferred dawn and dusk feeding times to return to the shallows to feed. In cool lakes, this situation may continue through the entire summer, while in warm lakes, a summer pattern may begin soon after spawning.

This stage-to-spawn-again versus summer-pattern behavior is driven by water temperature. If water around the spawning beds remains at appropriate temperatures, bluegills will often continue to spawn; but if it warms beyond their comfort range, they'll move to deeper summer locations, sometimes beyond the reach of fly tackle. Again, this is a function of the lakes you fish.

Shallow bays with sand or gravel bottoms and weed cover, in perhaps six or seven feet of water, are always worth a look. This includes areas where lily pads are present, if you can deal with lost flies and fish due to the heavy weed growth. Sheltered shorelines, particularly those with a drop-off to which the fish can relate, are also good places to check out. Points can also be excellent places to throw a line, as long as there is some weed cover. Small bluegills are not particularly spooky, so don't ignore beach areas, boat docks, or marinas. Docks, in particular, can provide excellent post-spawn angling.

Post-spawn bluegills are less aggressive than they are at the height of the spawn, and at this time, with a whimper, I put my little poppers away—except when it's almost dark. In low light (dawn and dusk), poppers will still provoke active strikes as the fish move into the shallows to forage. But during most of the day, I do my shallow-water work with conventional dry flies. Sizes 10 to 14 are pretty much the rule for me, and I fish flies such as Adams, Humpies, March Browns, Light and Dark Cahills, Blue-Winged Olives, and Blue Duns—just the sort of stuff that you may already have rattling around in your fly box. And I blush to

"The Critic's Circle." Watch out for gluttons and party crashers. Brad Befus

admit that I do make a rudimentary attempt to match the hatch. This involves peering at the lake in a bemused way and trying to duplicate the general size and color of the critters I see on the water.

It is at this time of the year that I begin to see what I call "The Critic's Circle." I fire my fly out to a likely place, and in seconds it will be surrounded by two, four, or even ten curious bluegills. And they stare at it. Forever.

They may be critiquing my tying (and frankly, I can't blame them for that), they may be analyzing my presentation, they may be talking over newsworthy events of the day. For the flyfisher, it is utterly nerve-racking. I have a couple of responses to this situation that are dictated by the actions of my critics.

The first response is to do nothing. I mean nothing. The situation is much like a group of party-goers staring at the last piece of pizza; eventually, someone will decide that he doesn't mind looking like a glutton, and he'll grab the pizza. In the case of bluegills, table etiquette is lacking, and when the first fish makes his move, his table-mates may decide that they're hungry, too, and several fish may charge the fly at the same time. Party crashing can also occur; be prepared for a strike from a fish that suddenly appears from an unexpected direction.

My second response occurs when one fish in the circle seems to say, "Hell, fellers, this damn thing is dead! I'm gonna go look for a snack," and begins to leave the circle. When this happens, the others will often agree, and the circle will begin to break up. This is the time for a tiny twitch, just enough to say, "Hey, I'm alive!" This often triggers a strike.

Summer Bluegills

The advent of summer will depend on the character of your lake. In southern states, waters may warm sufficiently (mid- to high seventies) to drive big bluegills out of the shallows and into deep water. On the other hand, in northern lakes, bluegills may be able to stay in relatively shallow water all summer long. In all but the warmest waters, you can usually depend on bluegills to return to shallow water to feed at dawn and dusk.

Large bluegills, in particular, will make the move from their spawning areas into deeper water in the summer. In some cases, this will mean far out into the lake in as much as twenty-five feet of water. This can make flyfishing for summer bluegills a grim proposition.

But in other lakes they may not have to move very far to find cooler water. If the cove in which they spawned slopes off quickly, they may be able to move thirty feet or so out into the lake and still have easy access to the shallows for feeding. In this case, morning and evening will provide fine bluegill fishing throughout the summer.

Okay, I'll admit it. I tend to be a lazy bluegill angler. I don't like to work very hard for them, and my summer tactics take my laziness into account: I fish only when the fish are active.

In late afternoon, I'll begin working the structure, weedline, or cover nearest the shallows. My logic is that the bluegills will begin moving into the shallows as the light fades, and I want to be there to cast to them on their way in. In cool lakes and where there is cover in about five feet of water, I'll be able to use surface flies and my baby poppers. In deep lakes, I may need sink-tip lines and small streamers and nymphs. And, just as was the case in the spring, if I'm catching lots of small bluegills in shallow water, it's always worth moving a bit deeper and throwing a small streamer or nymph for a while. Large bluegills are more prone to feed in a bit deeper water and to feed on subsurface prey.

As it starts to get dark in the evening, I'll move into the shallows, where I'll cast into less than five feet of water. The bluegills' feeding tempo will increase, and now I'll return to poppers and dries. This time of the evening is one of the best times I've found to fish for bluegills during the height of summer. Very early morning can be just as good.

How late you elect to fish is dependent on circumstances and your casting ability. On a clear night with a full moon, bluegills may feed long after dark. Brightly lit docks and marinas attract insects, and bluegills are likely to follow. On the other hand, I'm prone to put small flies into sensitive and inaccessible portions of my anatomy when I cast in low-light conditions, so I usually call it a night when I fail to tie a simple clinch knot six times in a row.

Finally, summer bluegill fishing involves a decision on your part. Do you want to flyfish as deep as the fish may hold? Personally, I hate trying to fish really deep water (more than ten or twelve feet) with fly tackle. In lakes where the fish move into deep cover, I'm likely to take my two hours of morning and two hours of evening bluegill fishing and find something else to do with the balance of the day. Fishing for largemouth bass comes to mind.

That's not to say that this is the only approach. For instance, Colorado is full of fanatic nymph fishers, and many of my friends appear to actually enjoy making long casts with sinking lines and weighted nymphs or streamers, waiting the eons it takes for the fly to sink to depth, and then s-l-o-w-l-y retrieving the fly with a mix of subtle jerks and long pauses. They catch fish. And often, they catch bigger fish. Different strokes for different folks, I guess.

Fanatic nymph fishers enjoy making long casts with weighted nymphs, and often they catch bigger fish.

Fall Bluegills

As the water begins to cool, the bluegill return to the shallows. Early fall is going to look a lot like late spring/early summer to both you and the bluegill. Final insect hatches will be occurring, crustaceans and mollusks are feeding heavily on dying vegetation, and minnows cruise the shallows looking for an easy meal. Continue to fish the shallows as you fished in late spring, but be observant. As shallow-water vegetation begins to die off and you notice less insect life, move out to deeper water. Fish weedlines, structure, submerged "stuff," and points and drop-offs. This is a good time to use fat swimming nymphs, small crawdad imitations, small streamers, and subsurface attractors such as Woolly Buggers and Prince Nymphs.

Fall bluegills continue to feed actively until the water temperature falls into the low sixties or high fifties. Then they move into deeper water for the winter, and it will be time to start tying flies for next spring.

Tackle and Gear for Sunfish

One of the reasons I began this book with the chapter on sunfish is that your existing trout gear is probably just the ticket for them. I've listed the equipment I use in case you're about to purchase your first outfit and want to use it primarily for sunfish.

Rods: I use a nine-foot, three-weight rod for the majority of my sunnie fishing. A rod heavier than a four-weight will probably be less fun to use. One-weight and two-weight rods are great for sunfish, as long as you can cast the weighted nymphs and small streamers that are sometimes required.

Reels: I use a premium-grade reel, but I do so only because it happens to double as a trout reel. Any inexpensive single-action reel will do fine for sunfish.

Leaders: Many, many sunfish have been caught on level leaders. But I fish for sunfish with tapered leaders, and I recommend them to you. A tapered leader will make casting more pleasant, you'll feel ever so much more professional, and when the sunnies are assembled in "The Critic's Circle," they may even comment on the delicacy of your tippet. Trout leaders are just fine for sunfish.

Lines: You're going to hear me repeat this about ten times in this book: save money on your reel first, your rod second—but don't even think about saving money on your fly line. It is the line that you cast, it's the heart of flyfishing, and it's really the cheapest part of your tackle. Buy the best you can afford.

Enjoy sunfish for what they are—a convenient fish near your home, a great fish to try for while you learn or teach someone to flyfish, or a passion.

For my sunnie fishing, a top-grade, weight-forward floating line handles the bulk of my needs. I also carry a weight-forward sink-tip line, but this is again because I also use it for trout fishing. Such a line would be a good investment for you if you want to go after fish that hold deep.

Flies: For surface work I like the conventional dry flies and poppers mentioned earlier. Often, sunfish will hang around near overhanging vegetation and pick off unfortunate caterpillars that drop into the drink. Sunnies will take other terrestrials when they're available, and a beetle pattern or two, a couple of hoppers, and ants are also worth having.

For subsurface flies (remember that big sunfish are more likely to be subsurface feeders), small Woolly Buggers perform very well. I like to use white, black, and olive for clear waters and chartreuse and orange for murky waters. The sunnies seem to like them, too. Small streamers and fat nymphs (dragonfly, damselfly, and Hare's Ear Nymphs and attractor patterns such as the Prince Nymph) also produce well. The new bead-head patterns have a definite place in your vest, since they'll get your fly to depth quickly, and the glitter from the bead generates strikes.

Sunfish are not very selective—it's one of their most endearing traits. Experiment with new ideas, use your tying bench mistakes, and enjoy the freedom of not having to match the hatch.

In all aspects of flyfishing for sunfish, it's most important to enjoy them for what they are. In some cases, they're a convenient fish, one that you can find near your home and use to keep in touch with the sport without a long drive. They may be a great fish to try for while you learn flyfishing or teach someone else to flyfish. The pursuit of trophy sunfish may even become a passion for you, just as it is with other species of fish. Whatever your flyfishing needs and desires are, sunfish often are best at meeting them. Enjoy.

THREE

SMALLMOUTH BASS

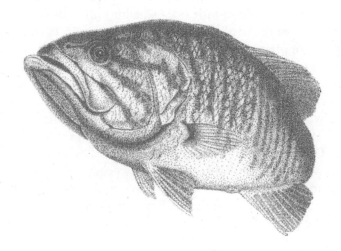

I nch for inch and pound for pound, the gamest fish that swims." Dr. James A. Henshall said it first in his *Book of the Black Bass*, published in 1881. I'm reasonably sure that a thousand writers have since filched that quote from the good doctor. Doc Henshall was absolutely right. Smallmouth are beautiful, scrappy, strong, acrobatic, and willing takers of the fly. For many of us who have made the journey "beyond trout," it is tempting to stop with the smallmouth.

Curiously, despite several books and videos on the subject, interest in flyfishing for smallmouth bass still lags far behind flyrodding for trout. I'm delighted. That leaves more bass for you and me to catch. Let's see how we might go about doing exactly that.

First of all, let's smooth the ruffled feathers of the ichthyologically inclined by saying that the smallmouth bass isn't really a bass at all. True bass include white bass, striped bass, and the wiper, a striped/white bass hybrid—smallmouth bass are members of the sunfish family. Closely related family members include largemouth bass, spotted bass, rock bass, and largemouth/smallmouth hybrids, known as "meanmouth" bass. Like sunfish and crappie, smallmouth bass are nesting fish, live virtually everywhere in the continental United States, and are wonderful quarry for the flyfisher.

The smallmouth bass (scientifically known as *Micropterus dolomieui*, or smallie, black bass, green trout, or bronzeback for the more casual) has two look-alike cousins: the largemouth bass and the spotted bass. The smallmouth can be distinguished from them by several identifying marks. The back of the mouth on a smallmouth ends in front of the eye (in the case of the largemouth, the mouth extends beyond the eye). Although color phases can vary, smallmouth also generally display three bands that radiate in a fan from the eye to the rear of the fish. In addition, they usually have nine vertical bands along the body, as opposed to the horizontal band on largemouth and spotted bass.

The world record smallmouth weighed 11 lbs., 15 oz. and was caught in 1955 in Dale Hollow Lake, Kentucky. This fish was a genuine monster. The smallmouth you can expect to encounter will generally run between two and four pounds and fifteen to eighteen inches in length.

Smallmouth are efficient and aggressive predators with acute senses. Where waters are clear enough, smallmouth are sight hunters. But the fish also have a well-developed lateral line sense and a penetrating sense of hearing that lets them hunt efficiently in cloudy waters. The thump of an oar, noisy wading, or the splash of a carelessly handled anchor will cause smallmouth to swim for cover.

Although originally found mostly in the eastern portion of the United States, the popularity of the fish has resulted in nationwide stocking programs. Today, smallmouth bass are found in most of the United States and many parts of Canada. Just about everyone has the chance to catch smallmouth. The corollary to this statement is that just about everyone does try to catch smallmouth.

But the flyfisher has several advantages. First, as far as food goes, smallmouth are as opportunistic as any other predatory fish. When they are available, crayfish usually make up the majority of the smallmouth's diet, but they also take advantage of aquatic insect hatches, terrestrials such as grasshoppers and crickets, and small fish or minnows.

This smorgasbord approach to eating means that the flyrodder can choose from a variety of patterns to entice strikes from smallmouth, tempered by the following consideration: they aren't called "smallmouth" for nothing. While an eighteen-inch largemouth might be able to gulp down a bullfrog of substantial size, a smallie of similar size might be doing well to swallow a little leopard frog. Spincasters and baitcasters can heave ten-inch plastic worms at largemouth, but a flyfisher can cast the smaller stuff that smallmouth like and that other anglers have trouble casting—things like small poppers and divers and trout patterns in sizes 8, 10, and 12.

A second advantage for the flyfisher is that, more so than other fish, bass are inclined to be, well, a tad cross-eyed. After a ferocious charge, they regularly miss the fly. A flyrodder is uniquely equipped to

They aren't called "smallmouth" for nothing. Flyfishers can cast the smaller stuff that smallmouth bass like and that other anglers have trouble casting.

pick his fly off the water and go back after a myopic smallmouth before its aggressiveness fades. This is a trick that no spincaster or baitcaster can pull off.

Smallmouth Habits and Habitat

Smallmouth bass prefer clearer, cooler waters than the largemouth and are more likely to be found in areas of rocky cover, rather than in the vegetation that the largemouth prefers, but there are plenty of waters where largemouth and smallmouth live together.

At water temperatures near forty degrees, smallmouth are torpid, and little feeding occurs until temperatures rise above fifty degrees. In the northern part of the United States, smallmouth are most active when water temperatures are in the low sixties to low seventies. But in southern reservoirs smallies may be active at higher temperatures, from the mid-seventies to the mid-eighties. (As usual, the temperature ranges here are averages.) There are a couple of explanations for this difference. First of all, the southern reservoirs are simply warmer, and small-mouth may have to forage at less than ideal temperatures. In addition, warmer overall temperatures foster the decay of vegetation, so the deeper regions of southern reservoirs may be oxygen poor, forcing smallmouth to remain in shallower water, where the water temperatures aren't what they prefer.

Because of their desire to live in comparatively clear, clean waters, smallmouth are also more likely to be found in moving waters than other members of their family. While they won't tolerate strong currents, smallmouth inhabit slowly moving rivers and streams very successfully. Many eastern rivers and lower elevation western rivers with slow runs, mild riffles, and pools are home to good populations of smallmouth.

In stillwater, smallmouth prefer areas where water flows into the lake or areas where currents flow along or between structures. They're usually shallow-water fish and will generally be found in less than twenty feet of water. Even if they're holding in fairly deep water, they'll often return regularly to the shallows to forage for food, usually in the early morning and in the evening. This helps make the fish accessible to the flyrodder. Often, they will be found in areas where shallow water offers rapid access to deeper water, such as drop-offs. Rocky areas, offering cover both for the smallmouth and its prey, are strongly preferred.

Like other members of their family, smallmouth exhibit fairly sophisticated spawning behavior in the sense that they are a nesting fish and the male gives at least some protection to the eggs and fry while they're most vulnerable to predation. Smallmouth nest in as little as eighteen inches to perhaps as much as five feet of water.

Before we follow them through the seasons, we should briefly consider the effect of the weather on smallmouth bass. One key to good weather for smallmouth is consistency. As is the case with most fishing, the state of the weather can improve (or degrade) smallmouth fishing, but a period of stable weather—even if the conditions are less than ideal—will generally yield better fishing than unsettled conditions.

With this in mind, other weather factors need to be considered. The day or so before the arrival of a storm can mark good smallmouth fishing. However, cold fronts, particularly during the warmer months, can bring feeding activity to a halt. During cooler months, particularly in the fall, this effect is not as noticeable.

Anything that produces low-light conditions will also generally produce better fishing for smallmouth. Cloudy days, rain, and wind can all improve your odds of success. A warm spring rain can raise water temperatures in the shallows, and that can cause smallmouth to feed aggressively. On the other hand, a thunderstorm with cold rain may bring feeding to a halt, and a severe one may affect fishing for several days.

Finally, the size of the lake must be taken into account when the effects of weather are considered. A small, shallow pond may respond to changes in temperature very quickly, and smallmouth fishing can turn off (or on) in a matter of hours. Large lakes take longer to respond to changes in the weather, and a brief cold snap or warm spell may have little effect. In addition, a large, shallow flat (even in a large lake) may respond to temperature changes quickly, while a shallow shelf that abruptly drops off into deep water may be relatively immune to transient temperature changes.

Recently, I had the opportunity to fish a small pond that held some fine smallmouth. On the first day of my trip, air temperatures were in the seventies, and I had a field day. Fish hit consistently and aggressively all day long. But when I left the house on the morning of the second day, the temperature had fallen into the mid-thirties, and a light snow was falling. When I arrived at the pond, I tied on a Clouser Minnow and cast. I had an immediate strike and landed a three-pound, eighteen-inch smallmouth. And that was the last smallie I was to see that day. The temperature never rose above the forties, the small pond cooled quickly, and the fish responded by moving into deep water where I couldn't reach them. Their feeding had slowed or ceased. Had the pond been a lake, I might have gotten another good day of fishing.

Anything that produces low-light conditions will improve smallmouth fishing. Cloudy days, rain, and wind can all increase your success.

Seasons of the Smallmouth

Unlike many fish, smallmouth that live in lakes are not known for making long migrations unless their food sources demand it. Indeed, smallmouth may remain at or near their spawning sites all year long, moving deeper or shallower in response to water temperature, local weather conditions, and the availability of food.

Smallies can live in virtually any sort of water, so before we begin our discussion of lakes and rivers and where the fish can be found in them, it might be helpful to divide the smallie's life into easily recognized segments that occur wherever they live.

Pre-spawn Smallmouth

Pre-spawn marks the beginning of spring for smallies, when the fish move from deep winter locations into shallower spawning areas. During this time, both sexes are feeding aggressively. Nest building on the part of the males commences, and fish of both sexes will be moving into spawning areas in the shallows. Surface water temperatures range from the forties to fifties.

Shallower lakes will naturally warm faster, so when ice-off occurs, begin your smallmouth fishing in smaller lakes and ponds. To maximize your odds of success even more, fish during the warmest part of the day and concentrate on the shallows. Keep in mind that dark bottoms warm faster than lighter bottoms, as well.

Spawning Smallmouth

Spring is well under way when the act of spawning takes place. Water temperatures generally range between sixty-two and sixty-five degrees. However, the actual time of the spawn may vary by several months, and the spawning temperature can likewise be considerably different, depending on the part of the country in which you fish. Males are generally either on the nest or driving females to the nest, and they are aggressive and will hit flies readily. Although some females will also take a fly, most of them have other things on their minds.

Nesting areas are usually located near an object that will shelter the eggs from waves or current (a log, large rock, or old tire). Sandy or gravelly bottoms are strongly preferred.

After nest building and spawning have occurred, a period of sulking and guarding commences. At this time, the males are guarding eggs and fry, and the females have retreated to deep water to recuperate—or sulk. The males continue to strike flies aggressively, the females are very tough to catch.

Immediately after the spawn I choose to fish for other species, and I'd like to urge you to consider doing the same. Bass eggs and fry are great sunfish food, and a guardian male that's been removed from the nest (or so stressed by being caught that it leaves the nest) simply can't perform its allotted task: the protection of the eggs and fry. Catching a nest-protecting bass today will do nothing to improve bass fishing tomorrow. I think fishing for nesting bass is unsporting, too, because they're so easily caught.

Post-spawn Smallmouth

In many parts of the United States, post-spawn coincides with the beginning of summer. The fry are on their own, the females have recovered from the spawn, and both sexes are feeding aggressively. It's also a time when smallmouth will exhibit their most stable behavior. If their food sources stay in one place, they're likely to do the same. Crawdads are homebodies, and if smallmouth find a good population of mudbugs, they're likely to remain in the area all summer long. Crawdads like areas of broken rocks where they can hide from cruising smallmouth, and if you find 'dads and rocks, you'll probably find smallmouth bass, too.

As I said before, smallmouth like to stay home, but if their food is on the move, smallmouth will also be highly mobile and can be tough to locate. In large lakes where minnows are the prime source of food, smallmouth may move miles in pursuit of them, so scouting, maybe with a fish-finder, is in order.

Smallmouth will also move to find water temperatures that suit them. In general, they prefer water temperatures of around sixty-five degrees. In the heat of the day, smallies may move from their normal haunts into deeper water. How much deeper is a function of temperature.

Early morning hours (yes, dawn) and late evenings are the best times to find smallmouth cruising the shallows in pursuit of the baitfish that are so abundant at this time of the year. Because you'll be fishing in low-light conditions, it's also the best time of the year for absolutely heart-stopping topwater action. Small poppers and divers produce well, but so will large (sizes 6, 8, and 10) conventional dry-fly patterns. Terrestrials, especially grasshoppers, become abundant in the summer, and a couple of fat hopper patterns have a definite place in your vest. Weedlines, lily pads, and submerged brush piles all hold shallow smallmouth. Mid-lake structures, humps, and extensions of points that offer shallow feeding areas and access to deep water are also prime locations.

Early morning and late evening are the best times to find smallmouth cruising the shallows during the post-spawn.

Because they're feeding aggressively, smallmouth may take larger flies at this time of the year than they do normally. This was forcefully brought home to me about a year ago when I managed to take a mini-vacation in Minnesota. I had no particular species in mind, although I hoped to get a shot at some big northerns and bigger muskies. During the heat of the day, I fished a shallow, rocky hump no more than five feet deep that was surrounded by deeper water and I began catching nice smallmouth with gratifying regularity. It was fun, but to me what was interesting was what the smallies were trying to take—seven-inch long, size 3/0 Bunny Flies tied for pike and muskie. I frankly don't know how they managed to swallow them. I did have a lot of short strikes, and when I switched to D's Minnows, my success rate went up dramatically. (There's another lesson to be learned from this tale, but it will have to wait until the next chapter.)

Although smallmouth are a tough, adaptable fish, there are limits to what they can stand. Water temperatures in the seventies and eighties mark a move by smallmouth into deeper water, sometimes beyond the reach of fly tackle. When this occurs, water clarity will make a big difference. In very clear waters, I've had smallies come up from ten to twelve feet deep to take a surface or shallow-running fly. But in turbid waters, I suspect that the smallmouth simply can't see a fly and are more likely to stay deep.

A cool rain can improve the fishing for a couple of days, but as a rule flyfishers would do well to fish during the cool hours of the day. During the heat of the day, smallmouth spread out over good habitat (deeper rocky bottoms, structure, old streambeds, and deep, rocky banks) and may stage at various depths. Presentation becomes very important, and if you intend to fish for smallmouth during the heat of the day, it's a time for experimentation with sinking flies, sinking flies combined with sink-tip lines, and finally, sinking flies combined with full-sink lines.

There are a couple of factors that can improve this scenario. When deep water is close to shallow feeding areas, smallmouth will continue to move back into the shallows in the morning and evening, when the water temperatures are at their coolest. A cool stream flowing into a lake can be both a food pipeline and a place where smallmouth can also find relief from the heat. Don't ignore areas of continuous shade, because when it's available, smallmouth will try to find cover that will enable them to remain in the shallows. Before you give up on summer smallies, take a moment to throw a fly near docks and areas where trees overhang the water and provide both substantial shade and ambush areas for hungry smallmouth.

Fall Smallmouth

When fall arrives and water temperatures drop to the sixties, smallmouth will return to the shallows to feed aggressively in order to build up fat reserves that will take them through the winter and make eggs and milt for the next year's spawn. This is lunker time, a time when you can find big smallmouth tightly grouped as they work the shallows. It's a time very much like the spring pre-spawn.

As the temperature continues to fall, smallmouth begin to move away from areas of dying weed beds and vegetation and are more likely to be found around old deadfall, inlet areas, mid-lake humps, saddles, and rocky points. The smallmouth will feed aggressively, but as temperatures continue to fall and turnover occurs, equalizing water temperatures and oxygen levels, the fish scatter and are genuinely hard to find.

Continued cooling will drive smallmouth into deep water. Warm days may bring the fish back into the shallows for a time, and it's certainly worth casting to these fish, but in my opinion, turnover marks the end of really productive smallmouth action for the flyrodder. You can sometimes extend the season a bit by fishing small ponds. In some cases, there just isn't enough room for the fish to go very deep or stray to areas where you can't cast to them. But when water temperatures fall into the forties, even these fish will become very lethargic.

River Smallmouth

Although I prefer lake fishing, that doesn't mean you will. Smallmouth do very well in many rivers, and they can be very accessible to the flyfisher. Smallmouth prefer slower rivers than trout. They like cool, clean water, moderate current, and a winding course with riffles and pools. In large, slow rivers, a lack of suspended silt is important.

In rivers, smallmouth must move in the spring from winter holding areas in deep pools to spawning areas. Depending on the river, this migration may be over many miles, and smallies feed as they pass through riffles and other areas of the river they may not typically be found in. Usual spawning areas are along the edge of the river, where there is little current. In larger rivers, smallies seek out sloughs and mouths of tributary streams. In all cases, gravel shorelines, rocky banks, and flooded timber are preferred as spawning areas.

After the spawn, just as in lakes, a period of active feeding begins. Look for smallmouth to be where they can find shelter from current and dart out to grab prey. Bear in mind that they cannot stand as much current as a trout: current margins, eddies, pools, bridge pilings, and other features that provide shelter from the current are all good areas to check for smallmouth.

Fall marks little change for river smallies. They remain in their pools and eddies, feeding more heavily with the approach of winter. Chances are you'll enjoy plenty of action and smile a lot. But as water temperatures fall into the low fifties, they'll begin seeking out areas where they can wait out the winter. This translates into deep holes—over twenty-five feet deep—with as much shelter from the current as they can get. In some rivers, this may again dictate long migrations, and you may have another crack at migrating smallies as the fish pass through shallow areas on their way to deep pools or even lakes. Once again, very little feeding occurs after water temperatures reach the forties.

Finally, considering the fact that highly oxygenated rivers are more likely to be good bug factories than are lakes, you may discover that river smallmouth are very willing to hit trout patterns, especially larger mayfly dry and nymph patterns.

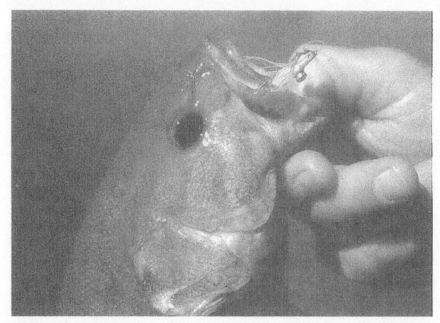

Although weighted streamers, such as Clouser Minnows and Zonkers, might be your first choice for river smallmouth, remember that they will often take standard nymph patterns.
Brad Befus

This is a lesson I have to relearn from time to time. Last summer, I fished a trickle known as Bear Creek, located almost in metropolitan Denver. I began fishing the spillway of a dam below a reservoir. I was fishing deep, throwing weighted minnow patterns, Zonkers, and the like. I was beginning to cuss the fellow who had told me that there were smallmouth to be had in the stream, and in disgust, I tied on a big mayfly nymph. A hatch was coming off, and I decided to chuck the whole smallmouth idea and try to pick up a trout.

I was to be terribly disappointed in my efforts to hook a trout. On the first drift, I picked up a seventeen-and-a-half inch smallmouth. And over the next hour, I caught seven more, ranging in size from two to three-and-a-half pounds. Before you think I'm smiling smugly, let me add a follow-up to this story. Although I usually fish Colorado's Yampa River for northern and trout, rumor had it that there were also smallmouth in the river. So, on a recent trip to the Yampa, my companions and I vowed to seek them out. We found an area where the river had overflowed its banks, producing something more like a pond than a slough. We weaseled our canoes in and were happily surprised to see smallmouth swimming about. We began casting immediately.

Did they take the large Bunny Flies that we were using for northern? No. Did they take any of the variety of larger nymphs and dries we presented? Again, no. What they did take were small, black Dahlberg Divers, about size 8.

There is a lesson to be learned here. Smallies are adaptable, and they will survive, even thrive on what is available. In rivers where minnow and crawdad populations may be sparse, they'll become bug-hunters. But where populations of small suckers and sculpins permit it, they will happily eat fish. Careful study of the forage available in rivers and streams is just as important in smallmouth fishing as it is in trout fishing.

Tackle and Gear for Smallmouth

When I fish for smallmouth, I'm usually keeping an eye out for one species or another as well. Sometimes it's northern pike, sometimes sunfish. My choice of tackle is often determined by what else I might catch.

Rods: In waters where smallmouth and northerns coexist, a heavier rod is helpful. But in ponds where smallmouth are the top-dog, sharing the waters with sunnies, light tackle will work fine. Compromises must be made (or you've got to carry a bunch of rods). For the angler who has decided that smallmouth are the prey of the day, I think a nine-foot, six-weight graphite rod is hard to beat.

Reels: Reel choice is dictated more by your fiscal health and appreciation of the machinist's art than the strength of the fish. Any moderately priced, name-brand, single-action reel will do the job for smallmouth, and you'll be able to make your next mortgage payment, too.

Lines: I like a bug-taper line for surface work, and I always carry a spare sink-tip line for smallmouth that may be holding deeper. If you decide that you absolutely must be able to go after smallmouth no matter where they are, a wide range of full-sink lines are also available. The difference in performance and durability between a premium fly line and an economy line is really day and night, while the difference in price is marginal. I recommend that you buy the very best line you can afford.

Leaders: For smallies, seven-and-a-half to nine-foot tapered trout leaders with ten-pound, 2x tippets will work fine for floating flies. Fishing in the rocks requires a stouter leader than is necessary for the fish itself.

With the expansion of interest in fishing for bass with fly tackle, many manufacturers produce special bass leaders, which turn over larger flies better than trout leaders. Shorter leaders between three and five feet long are the standard for use with sinking lines.

Flies: Dry flies are most effective during peak insect hatches on rivers and lakes in the spring and summer, and they tend to produce best during the early morning and evening hours. In lakes, giving the fly some action may bring more strikes. This action can range from a gentle twitch to more splashy routines; experimentation is the key. Dries are especially suited to those who may start their smallmouth fishing with light trout tackle. Try Humpies (Royal or standard), Adams, and Royal Wulffs in sizes 8 to 12. You should also have some terrestrials. These are land-dwelling creatures that have fallen in the water, and they are *not* happy. Active, struggling (as opposed to swimming) retrieves are in order. Try Joe or Dave's Hopper, larger Letort Crickets, beetles, and just for fun, a small deer-hair mouse.

Traditional bass poppers are excellent summer flies, especially in the morning and evening. Their splashy actions will often bring a smallmouth up from deep water. They make quite a racket, and the sound may also help bring a sulking smallmouth to the surface to see what's been disturbing its nap. Try small Dahlberg Divers (black, purple, or chartreuse) and cork or deer-hair poppers (natural, "frog," yellow, red, black, or white).

In my experience, the thing most beginners fail to do with these flies is to give the fish a chance to find them! Many, many strikes will occur on the *first* twitch, if the smallmouth has had a chance to get to the fly. This means that you should let the fly sit. How long? For the neophyte, let it sit too long—then double that time.

For subsurface flies, a selection of dragonfly, damselfly, and larger mayfly nymphs, Hare's Ears, hellgrammites, crawdad imitations, and streamers, usually in sizes 6 to 10, will get you started. You should swim nymphs in lakes, particularly damselfly and dragonfly nymphs. In streams and rivers, I like to dead-drift the nymph until it begins to swing in the current and then strip the fly back home. When you make that first strip, be ready! Crawdads are busy fellows, and I always fish crawdad patterns in a way that imitates their natural behavior. I allow the fly to sink to the bottom, keeping good line contact because I get a lot of strikes as the fly sinks. Then I retrieve the fly in jerks, allowing it to fall back to the bottom and rest between each retrieve.

Streamers are a long-time favorite for smallmouth, and I fish them shallow with floating lines and deeper with sink-tips. For deep fish, Clouser Minnows, D's Minnows, weighted Zonkers, and smaller Bunny Flies sink well. For shallower work, flies such as Woolly Buggers and Barr 'Bou Faces work well. A good collection of streamers would

Are smallmouth, inch for inch and pound for pound, the gamest fish that swims? Catch one and decide for yourself.

include Zonkers (olive, natural, black, gray, white, or chartreuse), D's Minnows (baby bluegill, baitfish, white, or black), Clouser Minnows (black/white, silver/white, white, olive/white, brown-gold/white, or chartreuse/white), Bunny Flies in various colors, Barr 'Bou Face (black, purple, or white), and Woolly Buggers (black to imitate leeches, olive, white, purple, and chartreuse because smallmouth just like 'em).

Are smallmouth, inch for inch and pound for pound, the gamest fish that swims? There's only one really good way to find out: catch one and decide for yourself. You might find that Doc Henshall had a point.

FOUR

LARGEMOUTH BASS

I n terms of the numbers of anglers who fish for it, the largemouth bass is the most popular game fish in the country. Virtually everywhere in the continental United States, in ponds, lakes, and reservoirs, large-mouth bass either occur naturally or have been stocked. Often these hardy fish have been stocked in municipal lakes, making them easily accessible to the urban angler who may wish to make a few casts on his or her way home from work. They are also willing, thrilling, leaping recipients of a fly, making them well worth a flyrodder's consideration.

The largemouth bass is the largest member of the sunfish family. The western border of their native range includes the states of Texas, Oklahoma, Kansas, Iowa, and Minnesota, while the eastern border of their original range included the states from Florida to New York. The popularity of the fish has resulted in thousands of formal and informal stocking programs across the country, which began over a century ago. Additional successful stocking programs have occurred in Hawaii, Mexico, Central America, Canada, Africa, and even Japan.

There are two generally recognized strains: the northern large-mouth (*Micropterus salmoides salmoides*) and the Florida largemouth (*Micropterus salmoides floridanus*). These two subspecies interbreed, as do their progeny, so there are many hybrids. Overall, the Florida subspecies is a larger fish than the northern largemouth. While an "over-six" northern largemouth is bragging material, it takes an "over-ten" Florida largemouth to raise eyebrows. The world record largemouth weighed 22 lbs., 4 oz. and was caught in 1932 in Montgomery Lake, Georgia.

Largemouth look much like their smaller relative, the smallmouth bass, but they can be readily distinguished from it. In the largemouth, the corner of the jaw extends beyond the eye of the fish. In the smallmouth, the corner of the jaw is directly below or even in front of the eye. The largemouth also usually has a dark horizontal band along the body, while the smallmouth has a series of vertical bands.

Largemouth vary widely in coloration. In turbid waters, they tend to be lighter overall than largemouth from clear waters. Colors on the upper portion of largemouth vary from pale greens or true greens through shades of olive, while their bellies range from yellow-bronze through cream and white.

Bass have acute senses, including the lateral line sense common to many fish. The lateral line enables largemouth to detect low frequency vibrations, and in some experiments, blindfolded largemouth have demonstrated the ability to prey on baitfish easily using only that sense.

Largemouth also have good vision, which is probably their most important sense in terms of hunting prey, and they can see colors. Unfortunately, experiments have failed to determine the colors that largemouth see best. Since largemouth tend to inhabit more turbid waters than do smallmouth, color may not be as important as size, visibility, and the rattling or vibrating characteristics of the fly. Recently, flyfishers have taken note of the largemouth's interest in vibrations and have begun tying rattle chambers (originally intended for insertion into plastic worms) into their patterns.

Bass also have a good sense of smell. Although they breathe with gills, nares (nostrils) are used to detect odors. It seems likely that the largemouth's sense of smell is used more for close-in prey identification (and during the spawning season to locate mates) than for the actual stalking of prey.

While I think catching largemouth on a fly rod is infinitely more fun than catching them on conventional tackle, one thing must be admitted: the interest in tournament bass fishing has resulted in an information explosion about the fish and subsequent technology transfers from tournament bass fishing to flyfishing (such as the inclusion of rattle chambers in flies and the trend toward dramatically larger bass flies).

An "over-six" northern largemouth is bragging material, while it takes an "over-ten" Florida largemouth to raise eyebrows. This one's a good bass anywhere. John Barr

Indeed, many second-generation bass flies are imitations of lures that have worked well for anglers who use conventional tackle.

As I mentioned in the smallmouth chapter, as flyfishers we have some unique advantages. For example, we can pull off a trick that no angler with conventional tackle can duplicate: with our ability to pick up line instantly, we can go back after a missed fish in a heartbeat, often while the largemouth is still fuming over its missed opportunity. Very often, making that second presentation will result in a hooked fish.

In addition, we can cast a wider range of food imitations—from one-and-a-half-inch crickets to eight-inch megadivers—than can an angler with conventional gear. This capability can be crucial, for although the popular image of a largemouth is of a fish that can swallow virtually anything, they will prey on small food items if they're found in abundance.

I also think that flies tied with natural materials exhibit more lifelike action, flash, and translucency than conventional lures. And in heavily fished lakes where largemouth have seen lots of lures, I suspect that our offerings *may* be more effective because of their novelty as well as their natural appearance, action, and feel. In the final analysis, it's important to remember that you and I are fishing for fun, and there is nothing more fun than a largemouth caught on a fly rod.

Largemouth Habits and Habitat

I mentioned that one of the flyfishers' unique advantages comes from our ability to cast everything from a bug to large baitfish imitations. This raises the question of what largemouth eat. Succinctly put, a largemouth will eat nearly anything it can swallow. And the aptly named largemouth can swallow just about anything. A bass fly must only be large enough to represent a significant meal to attract the attention of the bass. (It helps if it swims, rattles, splashes, or glitters and is within striking range.)

Preferred prey is other fish, and a largemouth can swallow a fish roughly half its size. But other targets—frogs, salamanders, crawdads, insects, and mice or other small animals—are not ignored. Even ducklings may be on the menu. Small food items are literally inhaled; the mouth gapes open, the gills flare, and the in-rushing water carries the hapless prey into the bass's mouth. This is an extremely rapid process and can be instantly reversed, permitting the largemouth to spit your fly out before you set the hook.

From the foregoing, it should be apparent that largemouth are less selective than are trout. Just as clearly, they are opportunists, changing feeding strategies and locales so that they can feed efficiently. In other words, while they prefer to use their huge mouth to eat one large meal instead of foraging for many small ones, they'll do whatever it takes to keep fed.

I was fishing at the Rocky Mountain Arsenal near Denver, throwing large flies that imitate baitfish but meeting with no response. All day I'd been batting inquisitive damselflies away from my sunglasses; there was a vigorous damselfly emergence in progress. Seeing regular rises, I

The aptly named largemouth can swallow just about anything, from insects to ducklings.
Steve Tofani

decided that if I couldn't catch a bass, I could at least play with the rising bluegills, and I changed to a damselfly nymph. It was as if I'd flipped a switch. The first cast resulted in a strike, and when I set the hook, it was like a bomb going off. Those weren't bluegills taking the damsels, they were largemouth! The nymph met with instant success, and over the next two hours I landed twenty bass in the three- to five-pound range.

There are two lessons here: first, largemouth bass are opportunists—sure, they eat big prey, but when an abundance of smaller prey
is readily available, they'll take advantage of it. Second, and perhaps
more telling, with conventional gear I simply could not have cast that
small nymph and caught these fish.

Largemouth are masters of a variety of feeding strategies. They
ambush prey from cover, they actively cruise for prey by investigating
likely areas of cover, they'll seek to fool prey by hovering nearby in an
non-threatening manner until lunch gets just a bit too close, and they'll
even chase down schools of minnows or shad in open water.

Largemouth can also be a social fish, if not a schooling fish. In
areas where hunting is good, largemouth are regularly found together.
This is very evident when they're chasing baitfish.

Like their relatives, the sunfish, largemouth are lovers of cover and
are more likely to be found in areas of heavy weed growth or deadfall
than in open water. When hooked, largemouth will use this cover to
their advantage, wrapping line and leader around whatever is available.
The end result is often a stand-off, with angler and largemouth glaring
at each other.

While superficially similar, the differences in jaw shape provide
some more clues to the differences in feeding preference (and, therefore, to predation behavior and selection of habitat) between smallmouth and largemouth bass. The jaws of a smallie meet nicely, almost
like a pair of tongs. They are admirably suited for grabbing crawdads
off the bottom. The lower jaw of the largemouth, on the other hand,
protrudes beyond the upper jaw and is designed more for engulfing
fleeing fish and snaring surface prey.

Compared to smallmouth, largemouth are a "warmer" fish. Feeding activity usually begins when water temperatures rise to about fifty-
five degrees, and peak feeding occurs from roughly seventy to eighty
degrees. As a very general rule, all largemouth activities (moving into
the shallows in the spring, spawning, and moving into water with acceptable summer temperatures) will happen in water that is seven to ten
degrees warmer than for the smallmouth. This is not a vast difference,
but it helps explain why, as long as suitable habitats are present for both
fish, largemouth and smallmouth can share the same waters.

Experts have many opinions concerning why the largemouth takes
a fly. Hunger is certainly one reason, but enough largemouth have been
caught with bulging bellies to make most observers believe that other
factors also play a significant role. Some feel that largemouth are simply

Learning to "read" a lake will lead you to beyond-trout species that can be easily reached with fly tackle. Chapter 1. (Photo by John Barr)

Doing your homework produces results. Chapter 1. (Photo by Bryce Snellgrove)

Weedlines and other structure provide cover for beyond-trout species. Habitat combined with water temperature will help you find fish. Chapter 1. (Photo by Doug Tucker-Eccher)

Sunfish are an ideal starting point in your journey "beyond trout." Chapter 2. (Photo by Doug Tucker-Eccher)

If sunfish weighed six pounds, no one would bother fishing for anything else. Chapter 2.
(Photo by John Barr)

Inch for inch and pound for pound, smallmouth bass are the gamest fish that swims. Chapter 3.

Smallmouth are beautiful, scrappy, strong, and willing takers of the fly. Chapter 3.

Largemouth bass are the most popular game fish in the country. Chapter 4. (Photo by Steve Tofani)

Largemouth bass are willing, thrilling, leaping recipients of a fly. Chapter 4. (Photo by Brad Befus)

When fishing for crappies, it's appropriate to keep the psychology of the fish in mind. Chapter 5.

Crappies are more "subtle" than sunfish—they're less likely to hit a topwater fly, easier to spook, and more difficult to land. Chapter 5. (Photo by John Barr)

Walleyes look like fish from Mars or fish possessed by an evil spirit, and for the flyfisher, there's an added air of mystery about them. Chapter 6.

The first time three-and-a-half feet and over twenty pounds of northern pike charges your fly, you're likely to join the author in his pike fishing madness. Chapter 7.

The sight of a dramatically marked tiger muskie over three feet long taking to the air—repeatedly—will etch itself into your memory. Chapter 8.

The last great untapped flyfishing resource in the country, the common carp has smarts and raw physical power in abundance. American anglers have been missing out. Chapter 9. (Photo by John Barr)

White amur or grass carp grow big, as big as king salmon, and are acrobatic champions. They may live in a pond near you. Chapter 9.

Favorite Beyond-Trout Fly Patterns

Clouser Minnow, Shad

D's Minnow, Shad (Tied by Darrel Sickmon)

Strip Minnow, Bluegill

Favorite Beyond-Trout Fly Patterns

Bunny Fly

Dahlberg Diver

Barr 'Bou Face (Tied by John Barr)

Favorite Beyond-Trout Fly Patterns

*Porky's Pet,
Deer-Hair Popper*

Calcasieu Pig Boat

Zonker

Favorite Beyond-Trout Fly Patterns

Clouser Swimming Nymph

Cork Panfish Popper

Whitlock's Crayfish

Favorite Beyond-Trout Fly Patterns

Dragonfly Nymph

Snapping Shrimp (Tied by Brad Befus)

Agent Orange (Tied by Brad Befus)

naturally aggressive, while others cite curiosity as the motive for a strike. Still others think the strike is a "wired-in" reflex, similar to that which makes a kitten chase a ball of yarn for the millionth time.

Seasons of the Largemouth

With these general observations as a background, let's follow the largemouth through the seasons to find when they'll be most accessible to the flyfisher.

Pre-spawn Largemouth

Spring and the active pre-spawn season begin when the water warms to feeding temperature, about fifty-five degrees. It marks a period when fish move in from deep winter locations to the shallows and begin feeding aggressively. Small lakes and shallow lakes, as well as dark-bottomed areas of large lakes, warm faster than other lakes. In all cases, you'll want to fish the during the warmest part of the day at this time of year.

I have a favorite lake that I fish about a hundred days a year. In the spring, largemouth use an old creek channel as a highway to take them to a dark-bottomed area. I'll sneak over to the flat around 11:00 A.M., and I'll have about half an hour of slow fishing. But as the sun warms the water, the largemouth begin to drift in, as if they were conjured up by a magician. I'll get an hour and a half, and later in the season perhaps two hours, of steady largemouth action. But when the water temperature drops as the sun lowers, the largemouth will vanish as suddenly as they appeared.

This is a fairly unique place because of the combination of a creek channel and the dark flats. But largemouth will consistently seek out warmer areas during the pre-spawn and will use fish highways, such as flooded roadbeds and canals, to access them. At another lake I fish, the largemouth move into a slough as the water warms, following a channel that's a foot or so deeper than the slough itself.

Lake waters warm gradually, over a period of weeks, and largemouth likewise become active gradually, moving in and out of shallows as the waters warm and cool on a daily basis. Because the warming process is so gradual, I think slow retrieves are in order for the relatively sluggish fish you'll encounter in early spring. I also think that small flies work best at this time of the year because they match the young insects and baitfish that are prevalent. Woolly Buggers are one of my favorite patterns to use because they successfully imitate, depending on their color, many things—a fat dragonfly nymph, a small crawdad, or a fleeing baitfish.

Spawning Largemouth

As waters continue to warm, the largemouth begin seeking spawning areas. They stage in cover or at drop-offs before they move into their spawning areas. You want to be on the lookout for shallow cover—weed beds, creek channels, timber, brush piles, and concrete pilings.

Largemouth become increasingly active and spend more time in the shallows now, feeding even more aggressively to support the spawn. The spawning process itself is a carbon copy of the smallmouth's. Like the smallie, largemouth are a nesting fish, and spawning begins when the water temperature is about sixty-two to sixty-five degrees. Temperatures can vary with individual fish and from lake to lake.

I have a good friend who has a dozen or so ponds on some land he owns. Many of them are home to good populations of largemouth.

Topwater action begins as waters warm in the post-spawn season. Largemouth come up readily to poppers.

Over the years, we've noticed that in two ponds, next to each other but differing in depth and bottom color, the spawn can be separated by as much as two months!

Like smallmouth, spawning largemouth are aggressive on their nests, which are typically built in water from one to four feet deep. Firm bottoms are preferred, because the presence of excessive silt can smother the eggs. Cover, which both shields the nest and reduces the area the male must guard, is also actively sought out. I hope you remember my comments about fishing for smallmouth during the nesting season in the previous chapter. Consider those comments repeated: leave 'em alone!

Post-spawn Largemouth

After the spawn, female largemouth, like female smallmouth, retreat to deeper water, where they spend a week or so recovering. The males guard the nest and will watch over the fry until they're roughly an inch long. At this point, all bets are off, and the male may cheerfully eat the fry he spent days guarding.

After females have recovered and males have stopped guarding fry, the fish become active again. Water temperatures move into the seventies, and largemouth seek out areas of weed growth for cover. At this time, largemouth feed heavily to overcome the weight they've lost during the spawn.

With the onset of summer, largemouth usually move to different locations. These can be quite variable, ranging from deep weedlines and submerged timber (between six and eight feet) to shallow, weedy cover. But the end result is a good one: the fish are still within reach and they're usually hungry. Early mornings and late evenings are generally best— largemouth forage in shallows at these times and retreat to deeper water during the heat of the day. Baitfish, fry, insects, and amphibians are abundant at this time, and largemouth take advantage of them.

Feeding can become frantic. Once I was fishing a lake right in the middle of a Denver suburb when I saw a commotion in the water. Initially, I thought it was a tiger muskie chasing minnows in the shallows, but after squinting against the glare for a minute, I realized that a group of largemouth bass were making repeated high-speed passes through a tight school of terrified baitfish that had had the bad luck to find themselves driven into the shallows. Were the largemouth actually herding them, as true bass are known to do with baitfish, or were they collectively taking advantage of an opportune situation? I don't know the answer, but a white Muddler Minnow fooled six of them.

The post-spawn is an excellent time to fish for largemouth bass. The fish lurk near weed-lines, lily pads, and timber. Doug Tucker-Eccher

The post-spawn is also an excellent time for topwater action, with largemouth lurking near weedlines, brush piles, lily pads, and other cover. Terrestrials are also abundant and imitations of them can be effective for largemouth. The ability to fish water six to ten feet deep with sink-tip or full-sink lines is helpful, particularly during bright sunlight or hot days, but you can avoid having to go deep by fishing early morning and late evening. When it's bright or hot, check out dropoffs, riprap, and dam areas where the fish have gone deeper to avoid the sun and the heat. Things that provide consistent shade, such as docks, tree overhangs, and moored boats, are also worth a try.

This fact was made clear during a trip to Minnesota in the dog days of summer. The largemouth were tough to reach with fly tackle, holding deep in perhaps ten feet of water. It was a fishable situation but wasn't nearly as much fun as catching largemouth on or near the surface. When I started flipping my fly under docks and overhanging trees and into areas where lily pads provided shade, the action picked up immediately. This kind of fishing is great fun. Casting accuracy is a must, because largemouth hold tightly to their shady cover. And when the strike occurs, you must take effective action at once, lest your leader wind up tangled in the prop of a large pontoon boat, resulting in the immediate freedom of a large bass . . . as well I know.

This brings me to the holdover lesson I mentioned in the last chapter. Remember those smallmouth I caught on that mid-lake hump in Minnesota? The largemouth I just mentioned were caught the very next day, on the very same lake, in very different locations. While there are many lakes that are shared by largemouth and smallmouth, it's important to remember that they are very different fish! As a general rule, smallmouth seek out cooler water and rockier, steeper habitat than largemouth. You'll find largemouth in warmer water and in cover that tends more toward weeds, brush, and timber.

Fall Largemouth

In the fall, the water begins to cool, and conditions are much like early spring. Largemouth return to the shallows, providing anglers with another opportunity for topwater action. But shallow waters cool first and fastest, and the shallow vegetation will soon die. As a result, largemouth gradually move out to deeper weedlines, both for cover and to be near prey that also seeks cover in vegetation. As a general rule, the largemouth will still be well within the reach of fly tackle.

At this time, largemouth are more likely to be cruising and will move away from areas of dying vegetation. They're more likely to be found near deadfall and inlets. Winter is coming, and largemouth are looking for large, meaty meals that will take them through the winter. Big flies (sizes 1/0 to 3/0) produce well at this time of year.

At the Rocky Mountain Arsenal, fall marks one of my favorite times of year. I work the shallow, weedy flats, throwing giant pike flies to hungry northern. But this is also the time I catch the biggest bass I get all year. It's a win-win situation: I catch either big northern or big bass. These bass take size 3/0, seven- and eight-inch Bunny Flies and big divers, and they hit them hard and consistently. The lesson? In the fall, big flies catch big fish.

Eventually bass feeding slows, usually when the water temperature reaches the low fifties. Just as temperatures approach this point, however, feeding can increase dramatically, particularly on the part of larger bass, almost as if the fish realize that they're facing the last call before the onset of winter.

Much of the largemouth's preferred weed cover has died, and the bass tend to cluster around timber, stumps, and the remaining weeds. As was the case during the early pre-spawn season, even hungry fish begin to slow down, so slower retrieves are in order. By the time water temperatures are consistently in the high forties, I've generally called largemouth fishing quits for the year. The largemouth are now deep and beyond easy reach with fly tackle. It's time to go back to the shallows and fish for fall northern!

Moving-Water Largemouth

I didn't call this section "River Largemouth," because largemouth usually don't live in the type of rivers that are common to trout fishing. Largemouth prefer even less current than smallmouth, and when they do live in rivers, they're usually large, slow warmwater rivers.

Even then, largemouth will go to great lengths to avoid the slow current that is present: Quiet backwaters are preferred year around and are strongly preferred as spawning areas. The fish that do live in the current seek out anything that will shelter them: bridge pilings, submerged timber and stumps, large rocks, protruding points, and the downstream sides of islands and shoals.

Living in these shallow backwaters, river-dwelling largemouth are highly vulnerable to being stranded by falling waters, and they respond to a drop in water levels by moving into deeper water quickly.

Heavier tackle is generally needed for largemouth, because the flies are too big to cast comfortably or safely with light rods.

Tackle and Gear for Largemouth

Heavier tackle than your trout gear is generally needed for largemouth, but not because the fish are bigger. The flies are too big to cast comfortably or safely with light rods. Largemouth flies are often tied on size 3/0 hooks, and heavier rods with their stouter lines will cast large flies much better. Also, as we've seen, largemouth, more than smallmouth, are prone to live in heavy cover and delight in tangling lines amongst the lily pads. Heavier tackle helps you strike hard enough to "cross the fish's eyes" and stop a largemouth's mad dash for the bushes.

Rods: I recommend nine- to nine-and-a-half foot, seven- or eight-weight rods—but in southern reservoirs with heavy weed growth, I wouldn't hesitate to use a nine-weight.

Reels: I'm sure you'll get tired of this advice, but here it is again: any good single-action reel is fine for largemouth. Since you'll probably be using a heavier rod, chances are you'll need to move to a bigger reel to balance your tackle.

Lines: Largemouth bass flyrodding is where bug-taper lines really come into their own. Trout anglers won't believe how wind-resistant big largemouth flies are—it's a lot like trying to throw a badminton birdie across the street. Bug tapers, particularly in the heavier eight- and nine-weights, help significantly to turn over big, hairy bugs. Again, I recommend buying the best line possible. I also carry sink-tip lines for big divers and streamers.

Leaders: I recommend special bass leaders for the same reason I recommend bug tapers—they turn the fly over better. When you throw a big deer-hair fly, you'll welcome all the help you can get. The test strength of your leader depends on your needs. While I think it would take a real brute of a largemouth to break a ten-pound test tippet, southern anglers who have to horse bass from cover may want to use twelve-, fifteen- and even twenty-pound test tippets. Western anglers who fish more barren reservoirs may do just fine with eight-pound tippets.

Flies: For surface work I like Dahlberg Divers, hair and cork poppers, and sliders in sizes ranging from as small as size 4 to as large as size 3/0. Black, purple, chartreuse, and white are all proven colors. Red, red and white, olive, yellow, and "frog" also work well. And for largemouth bass, weed guards on flies are like a certain credit card . . . don't leave home without them!

In terms of tactics, I'm going to sound like a broken record. Let surface flies sit. And sit. And sit. Keep your wits about you; with this sort of presentation, often the first hint of movement will result in an explosive strike, making the water erupt like a volcano. The eruption is the bass breaking water, its huge mouth gaping, preparing to engulf your fly. If you miss the fish, it's probably because you pulled the fly away from it.

Perhaps the hardest part of flyfishing for largemouth bass is waiting the half a heartbeat or so that it takes the bass to take your fly properly. Some anglers, cooler under pressure than I am, wait to feel the weight of the fish before they strike. In any event, don't forget to go back after a missed fish. If you can, pick up your fly immediately and put it right back where the water is still disturbed. Very often the bass will be right where you left it, wondering where dinner went.

You'll remember that I also carry sink-tip lines, and you probably wondered why I bother, since the largemouth I fish for are rarely more than eight feet deep. I do so because there is a sneaky technique, particularly well suited to searching new water, that involves the deadly Dahlberg Diver and a sink-tip line. The Diver is cast and permitted to rest. The sink-tip does its job, leaving the Diver floating. Give the Diver a short pop or two, to entice surface-feeding bass, and follow that with a long, strong strip. This sinks the diver, to draw the interest of bass that are feeding deeper. This is followed by a pause, allowing the Diver to resurface. Strikes often occur during the Diver's wobbling, slack-line journey to the top—be prepared. The process is then repeated.

Finally, topwater flyfishing is designed to attract the attention of a largemouth that is lurking near cover. Largemouth are reluctant to "blow their cover" until they're positive they have a meal in hand, so they often hold very tightly to their ambush site. This means you must work cover thoroughly and closely. A fly presented six feet from a likely ambush site may be too far away. On the other hand, it makes no sense to startle a fish that may be ready to feed. This means you should work your way gradually into likely holding areas. On your first cast, present your fly perhaps fifteen or twenty feet away from your target. On your second cast, cut the distance in half. Then work your way in on the next cast or two and eventually try to hit the bass on the head.

For subsurface work, Zonkers, Bunny Flies, Barr 'Bou Face, Woolly Buggers, D's Minnow (baby bluegill, baitfish, white, and black), Strip Minnows, large leech patterns, crawdad patterns, larger nymphs such as big dragonfly, hellgrammite, and damselfly patterns, and Calcasieu Pig Boats with or without curly-tails, all generally tied in sizes 1/0 to 6, have worked well for me at various times.

Baitfish colors, tied to match the local forage fish, are effective, as are more impressionistic offerings in black, white, chartreuse, and olive. Flies tied with rabbit strip, marabou, or thick, palmered hackle often produce well due to the motion created by materials that breathe. A bit of flash, in the form of tinsel or Krystal Flash, often helps. And as I mentioned earlier, fly tiers have stolen a page from the spincaster's book and have started tying small rattling chambers in many flies, both subsurface and surface patterns—often with excellent results.

With subsurface flies you're seeking to entice bass that are cruising in search of a fish dinner. These flies are often particularly effective on flats or in areas of weedy cover where lots of minnows are present. Casting in a fan pattern to cover the water thoroughly and active, darting retrieves are the order of the day, with perhaps one exception.

One of my favorite subsurface largemouth bass flies is the Calcasieu Pig Boat, invented by Tom Nixon. Although I've never met him, I'm convinced he's a clever man. Seeing conventional anglers slaying largemouth with the combination known as a "jig 'n pig," he developed a fly to imitate an artificial jig. Tied with chenille and acres of rubber leg material, Pig Boats come with or without a "pigtail" made of Tyvek. The fly casts well and presents a large, crawly, moving shape in the water. They can be retrieved with steady strips, but I find these flies to be most productive when fished like the "natural": the fly is cast, permitted to sink, and then retrieved with jerking, jig-like strips interspersed with pauses that allow the fly to sink with wiggling legs and waving tail. Many strikes occur while the fly is sinking, and careful line control is a must.

With all the emphasis I've given to big flies, I hope you haven't lost track of the fact that largemouth are opportunists. Hoppers, deer-hair moths, deer-hair mice, and rabbit-strip "snakes" can all provoke the explosive strikes for which largemouth are famous. For instance, at certain times of the year, grasshoppers are abundant enough that largemouth see them as a steady food source. It's always appropriate to carry hopper patterns in your vest. Use very short, abrupt retrieves.

Big moth patterns, particularly in the evening, also generate strikes. The down side of moth patterns is that they tend to be fragile, and they can be aerodynamically miserable to cast, their wings causing the fly to spin during the cast, eventually weakening or knotting the leader. Try them out, and if they work, change tippets frequently. Deer-hair mice can provide great fun, particularly in the evening and early morning hours. Use a fairly steady swimming retrieve while wiggling the rod tip. Speed is not a virtue (how fast does a mouse swim?), but panic is.

A largemouth will also happily eat a young water snake or garter snake when it can find one. I make snake flies with clipped deer-hair, painted foam, or cork heads. I add six- or seven-inch bodies and tails of green (for garter snakes) or brown (for water snakes) rabbit strips. A little Gink applied to the rabbit strip will help keep it floating if you think that's important. These flies are also fun to retrieve, and you can have a ball stripping line and wiggling the rod tip to give the fly progressively more snaky motions. The problem with these flies is that the tail can easily foul the hook, and I find them best used with lob casts into areas of cover. Short strikes are another obvious concern, and with snakes, it's

Whatever fly you use, largemouth are one of the most thrilling of our beyond-trout species.

worth waiting after the splash of the strike to make sure the largemouth has managed to get the business end of the fly in its mouth.

And in the midst of this clutch of various flies, there's room for yet another one. Since its evolution is a bit embarrassing, I haven't given it much of a name, but when I refer to it at all, I call it the Accidental Stick-Bunny. It's derived from Bunny Flies, the pattern that's so deadly for pike. Bunny Flies are basically a giant Woolly Bugger, with a long rabbit-strip tail replacing the marabou tail, and a palmered rabbit strip used in place of the Woolly Bugger's saddle hackle and chenille body.

I was fishing for pike, using my favorite Bunny Fly, when I saw largemouth break the surface of the water several times. It happened that I didn't have any surface flies in my vest, so I retrieved the Bunny Fly, squeezed all the moisture I could from the fly, and covered it with drying crystals. When I cast the dried fly, it floated stiffly and high, much like a stickbait or a Slug-Go. You guessed it, I "walked the dog" with my fly rod and had a field day with largemouth! I've since had occasion to repeat this trick, and now I often barber the palmered rabbit a bit, which I think it makes the fly even more effective.

Whatever fly you use, largemouth are one of the most thrilling of our beyond-trout species to catch on a fly rod. Its widespread availability makes it accessible to almost all flyfishers, but the largemouth's pugnacious nature, its readiness to take the fly, and its grit in the fight are the traits that make it one of my favorite fish. There's a good reason it's the most popular game fish in the country.

FIVE

CRAPPIE

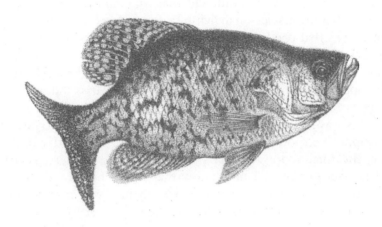

E arly in the spring, you might happen upon a few clever flyfishers quietly making their way to their favorite lake, pond, or creek back-water. They'll fish shallow water, using sinking flies and subtle retrieves. You'll see them casting into thick cover, working carefully and thor-oughly. And, to your surprise (because it's quite early in the season) you'll see them catch lots and lots of fish. The fish they'll be catching are crappies. Let a couple of weeks go by, and the flyfishers will have vanished—moving on to fish for other species. That's because, for the flyfisher, knowing *when* to fish for crappies is nearly as important as knowing *how* to fish for them. In this chapter, I hope to help you join the ranks of those apt anglers who have learned both the whens and the hows of flyfishing for crappies.

My first fly-rod crappies were utter accidents. Some friends and I were fishing at a local reservoir, casting small streamer patterns in hopes of entic-ing a rainbow or two. I was using a small white Woolly Bugger, and action was pretty slow. Suddenly, I had a fish, and so did one of my companions. After we landed our prizes, we stared at each other in surprise. We had each snookered a nine-inch crappie. We continued to work our way down the shoreline, and as the day wore on, we cast progressively closer to cover. We began to take larger ten- to twelve-inch crappies with regularity.

For the next week-and-a-half, we returned to our honey hole and continued to reap a bountiful harvest. Fifty-fish days were pretty common. But other fish beckoned, and to tell the truth, our hat sizes had increased noticeably. We were tolerably certain that we had the crappie figured out and were confident that we could catch them at will.

That was my first lesson in flyfishing for crappies: at times, they strike so obligingly that you believe you've got them completely nailed. But let a few days go by, and your self-assurance is sure to take a beating. They'll simply vanish, and all the wishing in the world won't bring them back. The crappie is not as accessible to the flyfisher as are bass and sunfish, and finding year around flyfishing for crappies may be difficult.

This was brought home to us when we deigned to go back after the crappie we thought we understood so well. After a day of flailing away, the final score read: crappies—two tired anglers, two tired anglers—zero crappie. I now know that the crappie we'd caught so easily were staging for the spawn or actively involved in spawning and were in water shallow enough to provide fine sport for us. When we returned to the lake, several weeks had passed, and the crappie had completed their spawning and had drifted off into deeper water for the summer. In the lake we were fishing, that made them inaccessible to fly tackle.

More so than the other fish I've discussed thus far, crappies are best pursued by the flyrodder by "fishing smart," and there are two ways to do this. The first is by fishing when crappies are in the shallows, at the time they're most accessible to you. The second is to seek them in places, such as small ponds, where there may be no really deep water and they're forced to stay where you can reach them.

Flyrodding for crappie can be a very pleasant way to spend a day or a quiet, moonlit evening. This chapter will help you target the times and places where you can fish for "papermouths" most effectively.

Crappie Habits and Habitat

Crappies are larger than their cousins, the sunfish. They also spawn earlier than other panfish, and they will often be the first panfish of the year available to the flyrodder. Like sunfish and bass, they're a nesting fish, the nests are guarded by the males, and they spawn in relatively shallow water. That's the good news.

The bad news is that crappie tend to be fish and plankton eaters, which means that they will often follow schools of minnows out into deep water or suspend in deep water as they feed on plankton. This can make pursuing them with fly tackle a pretty fruitless endeavor.

There are two varieties of crappies: black and white. Both are flat and have generally silver bodies. As is the case with most fish, markings on crappies vary significantly with the season of the year and water conditions; their dark markings, for example, can range from green to black. The males of both species darken during the spawn; black crappies can appear to be totally black, while male white crappies will darken around the forward part of the body and along the back.

All crappies tend to feed most heavily during low-light conditions: dawn, dusk, or even in full darkness. Bright days drive crappies deeper, and as you might expect, dark, cloudy days can bring crappies into shallower water.

Both blacks and whites have a large number of gill rakers, which permits even fairly large crappies to feed efficiently on plankton filtered from the water. They also pursue larger meals in the form of crustaceans, small fish, insects, and mollusks. Crappies rarely live longer than five years.

Crappie populations can fluctuate wildly, and a variety of theories have been proposed to explain why. One theory suggests that, once every three to five years, conditions are such that an unusually large number of young crappies survive. Due to population pressure, these fish grow slowly, and anglers catch small fish for two or three years. Once the population has been reduced by predation, angling, and natural mortality, more food becomes available to the survivors, and a year or two of good fishing for larger fish is at hand.

A second theory again suggests that every few years, an unusually large number of crappies are born. In this version of events, this large group of fish become dominant-year fish, and they subsequently prey, very successfully, on baby crappies from successive generations, driving overall populations down. But with time, predation, angling, and natural mortality again whittles down the population of the dominant year, more young crappies survive, and populations rise again.

Black Crappie

Black crappies are blotched or speckled irregularly on the sides and have seven or eight dorsal spines. The distance from the eye to the start of the dorsal fin is equal to the total length of the dorsal fin base.

Although both black and white crappies can share the same waters, blacks generally prefer cooler, northern waters and sand or gravel bottoms. Cover seekers, they tend to be found near vegetation. They also

Black crappie prefer cooler, northern waters. Cover seekers, they tend to be found near vegetation. John Barr

prefer quieter waters than white crappies and can tolerate more salinity than whites. Many observers feel that black crappies tend to school more tightly than white crappies.

The original range of the black crappie included most of the eastern United States, except New England. Through stocking programs, their range has been expanded to include most western states and some parts of Canada.

A one-pound crappie, black or white, is a fine fish in most waters, but they do grow much larger. The world record black crappie weighed 4 lbs., 8 oz. and was caught in Kerr Lake, Virginia in 1981.

White Crappie

White crappies have from five to ten vertical bands (which can be quite irregular) along their sides and five or six (rarely, seven) dorsal fin spines. The distance from the eye to the dorsal fin is greater than the length of the dorsal fin.

White crappies are more common in southern states. They can thrive in waters with either soft or hard bottoms and can tolerate muddier conditions than the black crappie. As a rule, they don't school as tightly as black crappies.

White crappie are more common in southern waters. They tolerate muddier conditions better than black crappie.

The white crappie originally ranged from New York to South Dakota and as far south as Alabama and Texas. Like the black crappie, they have been introduced in many western states, including California.

The world record white crappie weighed 5 lbs., 3 oz. and was caught at Enid Dam in Mississippi.

Seasons of the Crappie

Crappies roam the bounds of the lakes in which they live. They may come to the shallows to feed at night or on an overcast day, giving the flyrodder fine sport. Perversely, they can just as easily suspend thirty feet deep in sixty feet of water, happily sieving plankton from the depths, far out of reach of fly tackle. But there are times when the flyrodder's odds of success are reasonably high, and in the discussion that follows, I'll try to pinpoint those times for you.

Pre-spawn Crappies

In lakes, crappies become active shortly after ice-out, when the water temperature warms to the mid-forties. In search of warm water and plankton, crappies move into shallow areas, such as bays or channels. Dark bottoms hold the sun's heat better than lighter areas, and in early spring they'll draw crappies first.

Some lakes simply don't have much in the way of shallow areas. When shallow gravelly areas aren't available, crappies cluster around weedlines (the areas of the lake that spring to life first, providing food). The weeds may also create a firmer bottom than is available elsewhere. As you might guess, these fish can easily be scattered and tough to find.

As the story at the beginning of this chapter illustrates, these pre-spawn crappie willingly hit flies and are at depths where the flyrodder can fish for them effectively.

Spawning Crappies

Crappies spawn when the water temperature reaches the low to mid-sixties. Like sunfish, they prefer to spawn on gravel bottoms, but also like sunfish, they will settle for what they can get: mud, sand, or rocks. They seek cover for their nests in the form of logs, boulders, weed beds, or submerged brush. Cover becomes more important when the spawning areas are substandard, so don't ignore emergent vegetation or areas of flooded brush and timber.

Like sunfish, the male arrives first and builds the nest, but crappies are not as tidy a homemaker, and the nests are more difficult to spot than the cleanly swept sunnie nests. Nests are made in two to ten feet of water, with five feet being average. Some nests have been found as deep as twenty feet. White crappies often spawn a foot or so deeper than black crappies, and big fish often spawn deeper than smaller fish. Once the eggs are laid, they hatch in about five days. Unlike sunnies, crappies spawn but once a year.

The largest crappies may seek out mid-lake spawning areas, searching for structure like humps, piles of rocks and debris, or submerged knolls. This may place them out of reach for flyrodders who don't have access to boats or float tubes, and because these mid-lake features warm more slowly than sheltered bays, crappies that use these areas may spawn later than their smaller relatives.

Another place that crappies find the shallow, gravelly bottoms they prefer is in a stream or creek, and crappies will spawn in them if the current isn't too strong. As the water warms, crappies move deeper into the creek channels. Actual spawning is likely to occur in flooded brush and timber that provide cover for the nesting male as well as shelter from the current for the eggs and their guardian.

As you may have guessed, from ice-out to the end of spawning season is the best time to flyfish for crappies. The fish are found in shallow water, and they're feeding heavily to make up for the lean times of winter and to support the spawn. The nest-building males are also more aggressive than at other times of the year.

This may sound a lot like fishing for sunfish, but before you gleefully break out your fly rod, bear some other things in mind. Crappies like cover when they're in water shallow enough for you to reach them. In some areas, this can mean you'll be casting into areas thick with milfoil and cabbage—all in all, not so bad, although weed guards are extremely helpful. In other areas, it may mean that you're going to be casting into stands of submerged timber or brush, which is not so pleasant. Conversations with locals may save you hours of searching for spawning areas. Bass guides, in particular, are quite aware of what's going on in their lakes and, since you're not after "their" fish, may be willing to help out.

Once you find the fish, by all means look for nests. Because of the crappie's love for cover and their lack of tidiness, the nests will be tougher to spot than sunfish nesting colonies, but you might get lucky. As you're working a nesting area or a pre-spawn holding area, systematic coverage is the name of the game. Fan-casting, moving a bit, and fan-casting again is in order.

At any time of the year, it's appropriate to keep the psychology of the fish in mind. Crappies are, overall, more "subtle" than sunfish. By this I mean that they are less likely to take topwater flies, they will almost never strike as aggressively as sunnies, they're easier to spook, and the fragility of their mouths (from whence comes the name "paper-

The fragility of their mouths (hence the name "papermouth") makes it easy to lose crappie due to flies tearing out.

mouth") makes it easy to lose fish due to flies tearing out. The use of slow, bouncing, jig-like retrieves, imitations of minnows, nymphs, and crawdads, and gentle hook-sets are the rule.

Post-spawn Crappies

After the spawn has ended, crappies move to deeper water, usually near the entrances of the spawning bays. Here they often suspend in the depths and may be out of reach of the fly-rod angler. The larger fish that spawned over main-lake features will seek out deeper water between the spawning area and the first drop-off. Because these fish are out in the lake proper and are in deeper water, they're also usually beyond the reach of fly tackle.

As water temperatures rise, the fish move into ever deeper water, although they still seek out some sort of structure when it's available. Now we're talking twelve to twenty-five feet of water, where the fish may suspend. Maddeningly, they will also suspend over a featureless bottom if food in the form of plankton or schools of minnows is present. Hope of finding crappies when this happens is slim.

This move to deeper water is a problem only when there is deep water for the fish to move into, of course. Small ponds and shallow lakes can stretch the season for the crappie flyrodder.

Summertime flyfishing for crappies involves much research and some soul-searching for the flyfisher. Your decision about whether to try for them will probably be based on the character of the water you have available to you. If your crappie water offers deep areas, if you see the local bait anglers spending hours in thick stands of flooded timber or drifting slowly over structure in the middle of the lake, if the nice old guys with eleven-foot cane poles tipped with twelve-pound test and minnows tell you that they're catching their fish in twenty feet of water, you may elect to give summer crappies a pass.

But if you have access to some shallow crappie lakes in your neck of the woods, if you see those nice old guys moving their battered boats into the shallows in the morning and evening, if they're fishing with light spinning tackle, you may have a good shot at summer crappie action. Do your research, talk to people who really fish for crappies all year long (and there are plenty of them), and make your decision.

If indications are favorable, the morning and evening hours will provide your best chance of finding crappies in shallow water. You'll be looking for cover that supports minnows, small crawdads, and nymphs. Weedy areas, rocky areas where prey can hide, and areas near drop-offs

From ice-out to the end of spawning is the best time to flyfish for crappie, but the summertime angler who does research can still catch them on the fly.

or shallow structure are good places to hit. Crappies will also hang out around docks and other manmade features that attract minnows.

I've had some of my best summer crappie fishing late at night near docks at large marinas, using a canoe, boat, or belly boat. Usually the docks are well lit, which makes safe casting possible. As a bonus, the lights attract insects. Small minnows, perhaps reassured by the relatively low-light conditions, will come up to feed on the insects. The crappie follow, and they are often only six to eight feet deep (sometimes in as much as thirty feet of water) picking off minnows. This is fishing that is tailor-made for weighted minnow imitations. You should get your fly to depth quickly, and a bit of glitter or flash on the streamer is helpful. To me, this means Clouser Minnows, tied on size 6 or 8 hooks to produce a fly between an inch-and-a-half and two inches long. White Clousers produce well, as do imitations of the local baitfish, such as shiners and fatheads. Although crappies are certainly caught on dry flies, they're primarily subsurface feeders, and on a day in, day out basis, you'll be most successful with sinking flies.

Remember that the crappie is both highly mobile and a schooling fish. If you catch one, by all means go back for another! Count down as your fly sinks so that when you catch a crappie, you can go back to the same depth for more. When you stop catching fish, move. You may have to prospect a bit to find where the school has gone, and sometimes your prospecting will be in vain. But often the school has simply moved slowly along with its prey, and after a few moves along with them, you'll get a general sense of where they're going, allowing you to paddle or drift with them.

Fishing in shallow ponds is one way to beat the crappie's tendency to move into deeper water, but another option is to fish slow rivers and streams. At the reservoir where my friends and I had such fine pre-spawn fishing for crappies, we often fished the spillway below the dam, and we regularly caught trout, bass, and the odd northern or walleye. After striking out on post-spawn crappie in the reservoir, we started prospecting for them in the stream below the dam.

Immediately below the dam the current was too swift, but downstream the current slowed and the stream widened to include shallow, quiet backwater areas, and we again found crappies. They preferred all the cover they could get in the form of downed timber and the miscellaneous debris that tends to wash down any stream. But the big news is that there was no deep water available to the fish. They were within our depth window and were quite willing to take our flies. Like their brethren in the reservoir proper, these fish still preferred subsurface presentations in the form of white Zonkers and Woolly Buggers.

I hope the take-home lesson is clear: summer crappies may be beyond your reach, particularly when deep water is available to them. You really have three choices. Call it a day when the crappie move deep; move to the fastest-sinking line you can find and be prepared to wait the necessary century or so that it takes the line to reach productive depths (I would consider a boat equipped with a fish finder crucial to this sort of work—and I do mean work); or finally, once again elect to "fish smart" and pursue crappie in areas where they don't have access to really deep water—shallow ponds, lakes, or *slow* creeks and rivers that have thick cover in backwater areas.

Fall Crappies

As fall approaches and water temperatures drop, crappies return to the shallows, and the pre-spawn staging areas you fished in the spring can be great at this time of the year. Highly organized schools of crappies can be found along weedlines, and if the weedlines are shallow enough, this marks a second time when the fish are easily accessible to the flyrodder. This pleasant situation will continue until the weeds begin to die off. At that time, the crappie will begin moving out into deeper water near structure. Finally, when winter is near, the fish move out into the main lake where they will again hold, suspended in the depths.

Crappies also seek out the flow from feeder creeks in the fall. As temperatures drop they'll move farther up the creeks, feeding heavily as they go. Once again, they're accessible to the flyrodder—but get them while they're there to be gotten, because as temperatures reach the mid- to low forties, they will also move back into the main body of the lake.

Fall marks a time when crappies will again be feeding aggressively, and the die-off of vegetation (making it easier to fish) may make up for the fact that they're not as aggressive as they were during the spring spawn. Fish the pre-spawn holding areas using the same tactics you used in the spring, enjoy the action while it's there. When water temperatures drop and extensive die-offs occur, it's time to put your crappie gear away for a while.

Tackle and Gear for Crappies

Just how should you equip yourself for crappie? What we know about the fish helps us make some choices.

Rods: Because you're likely to be throwing weighted streamers and other subsurface offerings to crappies, I like slightly heavier gear than I use for bluegills. A nine-foot, five- or six-weight rod will serve you well. I prefer a six-weight because it will do double duty for smallmouth.

Reels: Crappies place no unusual demands on a reel, and any dependable single-action reel will be fine. If you're on a budget, the reel is the place to save some money. If your crappie reel will also be your smallmouth reel, a spare spool and ease of changing it will become a consideration, because you'll using both sink-tip and floating lines.

Lines: If you think your crappie fishing will be limited to the spring and fall when the fish are in comparatively shallow water, I'd recommend a first-class, weight-forward, floating line. But if you intend to try fishing when crappies are deeper, a sink-tip or even a full-sink line is necessary. Because I rarely fish water much over twelve feet deep, I use a sink-tip line. But if you're willing to fish deeper for crappies, I'd recommend a full-sink line.

Leaders: When they're in shallow water, crappies like cover. Really light tippets are out. I usually fish with six- to eight-pound tippets. Light bass leaders or heavy trout leaders from seven to nine feet long are fine. With sinking lines, I like short leaders, because longer leaders have a tendency to slow the sinking of the line. I tie my own tapered, three-foot, six-pound leaders.

Flies: Most of the crappie that take spincasters' artificials are caught on small jigs. Live-bait anglers do well with worms or minnows. With this information, we can make some pretty good decisions about what flies to carry and what retrieves to use.

A fairly good caster can throw a substantially weighted fly with a fly rod, and for some flyfishers, weighted flies combined with a sink-tip line and a short leader may be the way to go. A less skilled caster can cheat. Cheating involves using flies that resemble jigs—these can be either home-brewed affairs or more formal patterns. Bonefish flies, such as Crazy Charlies, and small Clouser Minnows tied with marabou instead of bucktail are about the right size and cast well. They sink quickly, look an awful lot like a jig, and usually ride with the hook point up, saving you from becoming tangled in the weeds. Bead-head nymphs tied in sizes 6 and 8, Woolly Buggers, small Zonkers, and crawdad imitations are also appropriate choices. Retrieves should be slow and jig-like. Many times, crappies strike as the fly is sinking and your line is relatively slack.

Boats: Crappies are highly mobile, more so than sunfish, and they're found in deeper water and heavier cover. In many instances I think

For anglers who enjoy careful presentations in technically difficult situations, crappies are a rewarding fish to catch on the fly.

you'll find that wading is not an option. A belly boat provides relatively stealthy access to the thick cover where the fish will usually be found when they're in shallow water, but it's really not suited to covering large expanses of water. A boat or canoe is probably the ticket for most crappie flyfishing.

Crappies aren't always easy quarry for the flyfisher, but they can be caught, particularly if the angler fishes at the right time of the year. The challenge of flyfishing for them can make the crappie rewarding fish to catch. For trout anglers who enjoy careful presentations of nymphs in technically difficult areas, flyfishing for crappies may be especially enjoyable.

SIX

WALLEYE

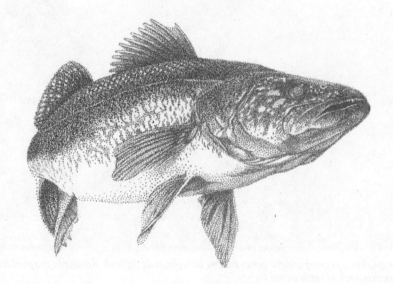

There's nothing in the world more eerie than the eyes of a walleye in the light of day or caught in a camera's flash. Their eyes make walleyes look like fish from Mars or fish possessed by an evil spirit. Sharp, recurved teeth and a spiny dorsal fin add to the walleye's almost reptilian air of menace.

For the flyfisher, there's an added air of mystery about walleyes, because flyrodders rarely fish for them, believing them to live beyond the reach of fly tackle. Tales told by baitcasters and spincasters of catching walleyes by bouncing worms along rocky, snaggy bottoms or by jigging in forty feet of water and, worse, of utterly fishless days when walleyes simply stopped biting for no apparent reason, have all helped keep this fish a relative stranger to the fly.

Some of the tales they tell are true. Walleyes can be a deep-water fish (in truth, even "shallow" walleye fishing is likely to occur in six or seven feet of water), and nobody disputes that walleyes can be very, very temperamental. But by fishing at the right time and by presenting walleyes with reasonable imitations of their preferred food, respectable numbers of fish can fall to the fly.

My first fly-rod-caught walleyes were the result of fumbling experiments. Years ago I routinely fished for walleye in the spillway area

There's nothing more eerie than the eyes of a walleye seen in the light—they make it look like a fish from Mars.

below a dam. Casting white marabou jigs with spinning tackle produced walleyes in the one- to three-pound class on a regular basis. The area I fished was reasonably shallow, perhaps ten feet deep at the maximum. There was a slight current from the dam above and the water carried food downstream to waiting walleyes. Better still, the current helped keep the water discolored, allowing the light-sensitive walleyes to remain active throughout the day.

The depth window was right, the fish seemed to be active, and during a moment of daydreaming an odd notion hit me: perhaps walleye fishing could be just as productive with fly tackle as it had been with spinning gear, given the right circumstances. Such circumstances, I reasoned, meant water that held walleyes and was shallow enough to fish effectively with flies and a fly pattern that would create the same action the proven marabou jigs did. The first two of these I had and the third I could tie!

Feeling more than a bit silly, I showed up one day with a six-weight rod and a floating line (I now know that a sink-tip would have been a better option), a heavily weighted, white Woolly Bugger, and a twelve-foot leader. My hunch was right. This setup produced walleyes on a fairly consistent basis. Throwing the fly upstream into the current, ahead of the slack water, gave it ample time to sink to the right depth before it hit the pool where the walleyes liked to lurk. Sometimes a walleye would hit as I dead-drifted the fly, other times stripping and hopping the fly back after it drifted through the pool was effective. I have since used this technique from Colorado to Canada, catching walleyes of up to eight pounds on the fly.

But no angler can ever leave well enough alone, and as the years went by, I continued to experiment with ways to catch walleyes. I still don't catch walleyes with the year around regularity that live-bait anglers do, but by fishing at the right times and places and by using flies that imitate the preferred food of walleyes, I like to think I catch my share! I think you can, too.

Walleye Habits and Habitat

The yellow walleye (*Stizostedion vitreum vitreum*) is the predominant member of this genus. A smaller subspecies, the blue walleye (*Stizostedion vitreum glaucum*), originally ranged in Canada and Lake Erie. It may no longer exist as a separate subspecies due to hybridization and polluting of the Great Lakes.

Close relatives of the walleye include the sauger, which is similar in appearance to the walleye but smaller (and with which the walleye can hybridize, producing a fish known as the saugeye), the yellow perch, and darters. Though often known as "walleyed pike," the walleye is obviously no relative of the pike family. Other aliases used by (or upon) the walleye include pickerel (an equally incorrect moniker), jackfish, and in French-speaking Canada, *doré*.

Originally, the walleye had a fairly restricted range, living in Canada and the northern portion of the United States. But stocking programs have spread walleyes across most of the continent, and the hardy fish does well in a variety of environments. You can find walleyes near the Arctic Ocean in Canada's Northwest Territories, in reservoirs near Phoenix, Arizona, throughout the Columbia River drainage in the Pacific Northwest, and across the country to the Gulf States. The walleye is extremely popular with anglers; it grows to respectable sizes and makes excellent table fare.

Like most of the fish we've discussed, walleyes can vary widely in coloration, from shades of golden brown in clear waters to shades of gray or silver in cloudy waters. The world record walleye weighed twenty-five pounds and measured forty-one inches. It was caught in Old Hickory Lake, Tennessee in 1960.

In the harsh world in which fishes live, survival often means having a trick or two up one's pectoral fin. Bass have the ability to engulf huge prey. Pike can virtually disappear in cover, from which they can dash with lightning speed to snare prey. Trout have learned to thrive in currents and on a diet of small insects. And walleyes have become creatures of the night, of shadows, of turbid, clouded waters, able to find prey when most other fish cannot. This ability rests primarily on three senses: vision, hearing, and the lateral line sense.

The walleye's vision is perhaps its best trick. The walleye is equipped with a special membrane in the retina of its eye called the *tapetum lucidum*. This reflective layer of pigment accounts for the walleye's uncanny *Night of the Living Dead* stare and serves the fish by gathering light to permit it to see well in low-light conditions. But everything comes at a price, and for the walleye the price of enhanced low-light vision is sensitivity to bright light and color vision that is skewed to the red-green portion of the spectrum.

Clearly, the walleye prefers to hunt at night or in turbid water. However, it's important to remember that a moderate chop on the surface of the water will scatter sunlight significantly and that the combi-

Flyfishers rarely seek walleye, believing them to be beyond the reach of fly tackle.

nation of cloud cover and waves can reduce light levels enough to permit the walleye to forage in the shallows during the day. I'll discuss the importance of light to walleyes in more detail later in this chapter.

The walleye also possesses excellent hearing, and in the type of shallow water where you're likely to be fishing for them, they will respond to splashy wading or the sound of a paddle clanking against a canoe with instant flight. Every bit of the care and stealth you use with trout should be applied to walleye fishing.

It is probable that the walleye's sense of hearing is used primarily to detect relatively high-frequency sounds (like that clanking paddle). Lower frequency vibrations, sounds that are more felt than heard, are more likely to be detected by the fish's excellent lateral line sense. In truly pitch-black waters (where the walleye is as blind as you are) or in very turbid conditions, its lateral line enables the walleye to home in on the vibrations produced by a swimming fish (or a vibrating lure or fly).

When they can find them, fish are preferred prey for the walleye. But like the other predatory fish we've discussed, they are, above all, opportunists. When fish dinners are lacking, they'll feed on insects, leeches, crawdads, and frogs. At certain times of the year, walleyes feed very heavily on mayflies, and if you're fortunate enough to be on the spot (more a matter of luck than skill, I'm afraid), excellent dry-fly action for walleyes can be had.

The walleye's preference for fish can work for or against the fly-fisher. In lakes where the forage fish feed in shallow waters at night or move in during low-light conditions, walleyes may be available to the flyrodder on a regular basis. But in lakes where the forage fish live in deep water, walleyes will follow them and may be available only to wire-line and downrigger anglers.

The abundance or lack of forage fish also contributes to the availability of walleyes in another fashion. In the spring, baitfish are hard to find. Overall food availability is low, and walleyes respond by cruising for food. They're hungry and hit aggressively. But as spring moves into summer, the forage fish grow larger and more numerous and walleyes can eat very well, indeed. A walleye with a full belly is less likely to snap at your fly.

Food fuels growth, and it should come as no surprise that the walleye's growth rate is determined both by food and the length of the growing season. In lakes where food is abundant and the growing season lasts over half a year, walleyes can exceed twelve pounds in five or six years. But in colder lakes or in lakes where food is not as abundant, a five-year-old walleye may weigh just a couple of pounds. Female walleyes grow faster, grow to larger sizes, and live longer than the males. A four-pound male walleye is a big fish.

In cool, northern lakes, walleyes can live over twenty years, and they will ultimately match the size of their faster growing cousins that live in warm, southern waters. Walleyes that live in warm waters pay for their explosive growth rates with lives about half as long as walleyes that live in cool climes.

Although strictly classified as a cool-water fish, walleyes can tolerate a wide range of conditions. Preferred water temperatures are in the sixty-five to seventy-five degree range, but walleyes will leave water in this range if food availability dictates or light levels become too intense.

Seasons of the Walleye

With this general information in hand, it's now time to zero in on the walleye fishing opportunities that are hot and to become aware of those that are not.

Pre-spawn Walleyes

You have to beat the robins to spring if you want to catch pre-spawn walleye. The males begin moving in to staging areas first, often when the water temperatures are barely above freezing. In some lakes you may actually miss the males because the water is still ice-covered (or because fishing in freezing water with the waders you forgot to patch last year is no fun). The larger females move in after the males, often weeks later. At this time both sexes are still in comparatively deep water.

At this time of the year both sexes will sulk until just before the spawn. But within a week or so of the spawn proper, walleyes begin moving into the shallows. This move is a gradual one, characterized by feeding in the shallows at night or during a cloudy day, followed by retreats into deeper water during bright-light conditions. As the spawn approaches, walleyes spend more and more time in the shallows.

Because walleyes have some pretty tough requirements for spawning (current, hard bottoms, low-light conditions), in many parts of the country they may use the same spawning areas from year to year. Local inquiries can be very helpful—as can a quick referral to your local fishing regulations. In many areas, walleye spawning areas are closed to fishing until after the spawn is complete.

In early season, you'll be using weighted flies and sink-tip lines for the pre-spawn walleyes.

If you find a likely area or if a kind person actually shows you one and you're permitted to fish it, you'll be using sink-tip lines to cast subsurface flies. (I hope you intend to release the pre-spawn fish you're going to be catching.) It's important to use sink-tip lines at this time of year. These pre-spawn fish still aren't all that active, they haven't moved into really shallow water, and you'll want to maximize your odds of success by getting your fly quickly to productive depths (from five feet to as much as ten feet) and by keeping it at those depths as long as possible. A sink-tip line is the ticket.

Fish the "edges." By this I mean the first abrupt drop-off adjacent to a more gently sloping area of riprap (this sort of structure is often seen along dams), the edge of a deep area leading into a saddle, or perhaps the edge of a drop-off next to a rocky, windswept shoal. The intent is to present your fly to walleyes staging in these areas, awaiting the opportunity (warming water, low light) to move into the shallows.

You should also fish the shallows themselves, those one- to five- or six-foot depths where spawning will occur, covering the water thoroughly to catch the attention of fish that are actually moving in to feed or spawn.

I find that either minnow or jig-like flies produce well for me at this time of the year. Weighted Woolly Buggers in white, black, brown, and olive are good bets. Clouser Minnows (which have the virtues of sinking like a stone, riding with the hook point up over the rugged bottoms walleyes prefer, and presenting a wonderfully translucent minnow silhouette) are also fine flies to try. All-white, blue-and-white, chartreuse-and-white, silver-and-white, and gold-and-white Clousers have all produced well for me, with all-white, blue-and-white, and chartreuse-and-white being probably the best producers overall.

Your retrieves and presentations should be tailored to comparatively sluggish fish. This means working likely areas thoroughly, making sure you're running your fly at a variety of depths, counting down to be sure, and using very slow retrieves.

Be sure to keep your safety in mind. You'll be spending a lot of time in deep water or in areas, such as a dam face or water right next to a drop-off, where one step forward may equal a couple more feet of depth. The water will be *cold*, probably in the forties. If you intend to wade, the presence of a buddy is the bare minimum for safety. Consider the use of a good personal flotation device; inflatable suspenders are now made with the wading angler in mind. The weather is likely to be blustery, as well. Belly boaters will want to be able to make it to shore quickly, and users of small boats and canoes should keep an eye on the sky.

Spawning Walleyes

Throughout this book, I've tried to give you fairly specific guidelines for when the fish we've been discussing spawn. There had to be an exception, and walleyes are exactly that. Because of their great adaptability, water temperatures when walleye spawn range from the low to mid-forties in the northern part of their range to the low to mid-fifties in the southern part. To confound the issue, some walleyes find the aerated water they need for spawning in streams, and spawning there can occur several weeks earlier than spawning in the main body of a lake. And, to add icing to an already confused cake, walleyes that spawn over shallow mid-lake structure can spawn several weeks *later* than their colleagues that spawn along the shallow shoreline. Although you've heard me say it many times before, it will serve you well to pay special attention this time: local inquiries are a great help.

The timing of the spawn may be tough to determine, but walleyes have special requirements for their nurseries. Finding areas that meet these requirements can reduce the magnitude of the problem to some extent. Preferred walleye spawning areas range between one foot and perhaps five feet in depth and feature rocky bottoms. Walleye eggs must be aerated constantly, so in a very real sense you're looking for exactly the types of places that the fish we've examined thus far avoid: windswept, rocky shoals; the riprap along dam faces, bridge supports, or lake-side construction; and shallow, rocky, hard-bottomed saddles between islands or an island and the shore, where prevailing winds can induce a current.

The males come in first, followed by the females. Because female walleyes don't all ripen at the same time, spawning will last for a couple of weeks, and both sexes feed during the spawn. Following the spawn, females retreat to deeper water for a couple of weeks to recuperate, while males remain in the shallows and continue feeding.

The retreat of the larger female walleyes is an important signpost, for when they return, one of the best times for the flyfisher to pursue walleyes is at hand.

If you elect to fish during the spawn, the tactics and flies you'll use are basically the same as the pre-spawn tactics and flies I've described above. I favor giving spawning walleyes (and most other fish) a break. You object to being interrupted at certain tender moments, and I can only assume that walleyes do, too. Spawning is the event that determines how many walleyes will be around for you to catch in a few years, and it's in your interest to let the fish get the job done as efficiently as possible. This is a nice time to check weedy flats for post-spawn northern or to see if smallmouth are starting to stage in shallow water.

Post-spawn Walleyes

Post-spawn is the time after the females return to the shallows but before the walleyes move into a summer pattern. Unfortunately, the walleye's ability to adapt to local conditions makes it tough to list hard and fast temperature ranges, but as a general rule I think you'll find that walleyes are in a post-spawn pattern when water temperatures range from the low fifties to the low sixties.

This is a good time for the walleye flyfisher. Water temperatures are still fairly cool, and overall light levels remain comparatively low because the spring sun is still hitting the water at a reasonably low angle. These environmental circumstances permit walleyes to remain in the shallows. Better still, forage fish and newly hatched fry are numerous and are available in a variety of sizes, meaning that walleyes won't be as selective.

Post-spawn is a good time for the walleye flyfisher. The fish remain in the shallows, hunting aggressively for food.

Walleyes hunt aggressively for food during the post-spawn. They'll cruise the shallow waters in which they spawned out to perhaps ten feet in depth—still within your reach, in other words. Points, reefs, saddles between the shore and an island, and shallow weed beds are all good places to check out, as are bays and flats. If they fall within your depth window, mid-lake humps and bumps can also be very productive. As walleyes end their post-spawn behavior, these mid-lake areas become even more desirable locales because they often offer immediate access to the deep, cool, dark waters that walleyes prefer in summer.

This is the time to be Johnny-on-the-spot, because while all this is good news for you, a variety of things are happening that are working against you. Each day the water warms just a bit. Each day the sun shines a bit longer and, more significantly, penetrates the water a bit more. Each day the forage fish are a little larger, thus reducing the time the walleye need to be actively feeding. Consequently, each day, the shallows become a bit more unpleasant for walleyes and their need to be there is less pressing.

With our trusty thermometers, we can measure how much warmer the water is becoming. It's more difficult to judge the brightness of the light in the water. Spring and fall, for example, can both be times of bright, sunny days for you but not for the walleye. The sun never gets very high in the sky at these times of year, and its rays strike the water at a more acute angle. More of its rays are reflected, and overall light levels for the walleyes are reduced, permitting them to remain in the shallows. On an overcast summer day, on the other hand, the walleyes may actually see more light than they do on a clear spring day.

Other factors also alter light levels for walleyes. Waves and chop roughen the water surface, and the sun's rays cannot penetrate it as well. Walleyes may therefore be able to forage in the shallows on a day that you perceive to be brightly lit. On the downwind side of a lake, this situation may be even more pronounced, because waves lapping against the shore stir up mud. A choppy water surface, combined with some turbidity in the water, can encourage feeding in the shallows.

More so than with the other species I've been discussing, light will be a crucial factor in your walleye fishing, particularly in the post-spawn season. You should always take its presence or absence into account, remembering that it is not the light *you* see but the light that the walleye sees that is important.

During the post-spawn, you're looking for fish factories like those I described above: relatively shallow environments offering cover and food for baitfish and a smorgasbord for cruising walleyes. You should arrive at these areas early or late in the day. The hour or so before sunrise, the hour or so after sunset, and night fishing are the most productive for the flyrodder after walleyes. As we've seen above, cloudy days and the action of wind and waves produce mudlines that can invite walleyes back to the shallows, providing occasional midday sport.

You'll be throwing sinking flies, and the flies I mentioned above will work fine. Although those flies will probably be the mainstays of your arsenal, there are some additions you might want to consider, such as a couple of crawdad patterns, a leech imitation, and perhaps some large, fat nymphs.

Circumstances will be gradually combining to persuade the walleyes to move away from water depths you prefer to fish. At the start of post-spawn walleye flyfishing, you may do very well in three feet of water. For this early-season fishing, your floating line will work fine, but this situation won't last. You'll have to follow the walleyes out into deeper water. At this time, sink-tip or full-sink lines come into their own.

Finally, you'll have to balance your desire to catch walleyes with the difficulty of fishing deep water. In my case, it's a matter of return on investment. Will I invest the time necessary to fish deep water when the potential return is an eight-ounce perch? Nope. A two-pound walleye? Probably not. A five-pound walleye? Hmmm . . . maybe.

Summer Walleyes

In summer, water temperatures and light levels both rise enough to compel walleyes to spend most of their day in deep water. Walleyes are most active in water between sixty-five and seventy-five degrees, and we already know that they like low light levels. We also know that by this time, baitfish numbers are high and they're as big as they're going to get, so walleyes don't have to spend as much time looking for food.

In some lakes in the North, the walleye may not have to move very far in depth or in distance to be comfortable, and baitfish and yellow perch may be shallow, as well. But in other lakes summer walleyes may be following schools of shad or ciscoes in very deep water. River or creek inlets that are cooler than the main portion of the lake may also hold walleyes. In any event, if you elect to pursue summer walleyes, you're likely to be fishing even deeper than you were during post-spawn.

With the walleye deep and the available meals numerous, making walleyes more selective, this is the toughest time of the year for the flyrodder in search of walleye. Fishing a shallow lake may help, since the

Low light and available food may keep walleyes in water shallow enough for fly tackle, even in summer.

fish may still be at a depth you can reach. But this is less than ideal habitat, and often the walleye will be small. Walleyes do best in large lakes or reservoirs with deep water, so this summer tactic doesn't work as well as it does for other beyond-trout species. In other lakes, the available forage fish may remain in the shallows, again forcing walleyes to remain in shallower water than they prefer. Here, though, the walleyes have a final card to play. Because of their excellent night vision, they may forage only during very low-light conditions, and fishing for them may require late nights or very early mornings.

Your best bet may be to fish for summer walleyes in rivers, where temperatures are often cooler, and there isn't any really deep water. We'll discuss river walleyes later in this chapter.

To be honest, given the choice of dragging a Clouser Minnow around in twenty-five feet of water or throwing a popper to a hungry bass, I'll take the bass every time. I don't deliberately fish for summer walleye, but sometimes I sort of blunder into it. Given a moonlit summer night and seasonable weather, I'll often fish into the night. Usually, I'm throwing poppers at bass and bluegills. As darkness increases and topwater action slows, I'll switch to a streamer. On quite a few occasions, I've hooked cruising walleyes that have taken advantage of darkness and cooling waters to forage in the shallows. If the shallows are still too warm, the first drop-off adjacent to a dam, embankment, saddle, or point is the place to be.

There is another summer phenomenon that's worth taking advantage of if you happen come across it. On several of the lakes I fish, there are heavy emergences of a two-inch long, pale green mayfly in mid-summer. These hatches seem to be heaviest during very still, dark nights. In Minnesota, similar hatches of a large brown mayfly can occur during the day. Walleyes prey very successfully on these insects, and in the case of the night emergers, their excellent night vision enables them to pretty well corner the market. When these hatches occur, walleyes often have a field day (or is it a field night?) on the emergers and duns. I fish large, light-colored mayfly dun imitations, and when everything is just right, I catch a lot of walleyes.

In lakes where these emergences are heavy and last a week or two, walleyes gorge on the nymphs, the emerging duns, and the spinners. They actually feed on these insects to the exclusion of other prey, and since this activity occurs at night or early morning, daytime anglers often conclude that the walleyes just aren't hitting. Nothing could be further from the truth. Cast and enjoy!

Fall Walleyes

Fall marks a temporary resurgence of fly-rod action for walleyes in the shallows. The sun isn't penetrating the water as well, as was the case in the spring, and water temperatures are declining. Better still, forage fish populations have been whittled down by predation, and while the individual fish are large, there are fewer of them. This means that walleyes have to work harder for food.

Of course, walleyes still prefer low-light conditions even with the lower angle of the sun. One fall fishing trip, I found myself out on a blustery Colorado day. The sky was dotted with thick, but scattered clouds, and I was throwing Clouser Minnows in hopes of catching trout foraging in the shallows.

About every half-hour, a cloud would cover the sun, and as though someone had flipped a switch, I'd start catching walleyes. The action was fast, about one fish for every two or three casts, and I had a ball until the sun moved out from behind the cloud. Just as suddenly as it started, the walleye action would stop. I spent about six hours on the water and benefited from about ten periods of solid, exciting walleye action.

As water temperatures fall into the sixties, walleyes move back into the shallows, *if* their forage fish do the same. That's a pretty big *if*, because even if perch and other baitfish move back into the shallows, shad and ciscoes may not. Depending on where you fish, the walleye's return to the shallows may last a very short time. In cool climates and in lakes that cool quickly, the return to the shallows can be over and done with in a week or so. In other areas, walleyes may simply follow their prey into deeper water, never coming back into the shallows at all.

Seek out areas that were productive in the spring and post-spawn seasons, but your efforts should be tempered with the following considerations. Vegetation in the shallows dies off first, and the forage fish lose these sources of food and cover first. Areas of deeper vegetation survive longer, so just as you did during the post-spawn season, you'll gradually be working your way into deeper water as the season progresses.

In addition, bear in mind that areas that hold heat longest remain active longest and, therefore, hold walleyes longest. Flats that warm quickly in the sun, dark bottoms, and warm creek inlets can all hold walleyes longer than windswept points or saddles.

Because food fish are bigger, your flies can be bigger at this time of the year, too. Clousers and Bunny Flies can be three to four inches in length, as can your leech imitations. Since walleyes are feeding heavily, the challenge you face revolves more around locating fish than persuading them to strike.

Turnover usually marks the end of flyrodding for walleyes in lakes. Like other fish, they scatter at this time and usually will not return to

Fall may bring a resurgence of fly-rod action for walleyes, but it will be temporary and will depend on the movement of forage fish.

the shallows until the following spring. In rivers, where there is no turnover, walleye action can continue longer, and rivers may be your best source of late-season walleyes.

River Walleyes

Walleyes can prosper in rivers, and during the summer and fall, rivers are probably the best place for a fanatic walleye flyrodder to be. Often, rivers are more turbid, cooler, and shallower than lakes. Although walleyes can live in rivers, they aren't a trout, and they will seek shelter from the current. In large rivers, check out features that break up current. Bridges and pilings are just as likely to be used by walleyes as more natural features, such as boulders. River-dwelling walleyes spawn in tailwaters or along rocky banks in the river.

Since it is more constant, water temperature is not the driving factor in rivers that it is in lakes, but the light level certainly is. Big rivers may offer enough depth for the walleye to hide beyond the flyrodder's reach during summer. But just as in lakes, a cloudy day, some chop on the surface, or an increased release of water from a dam that causes the river to become cloudy will permit walleyes to return to shallow water to feed. A release of cool waters from the bottom of the lake can also reduce water temperatures in the river, drawing walleyes into shallow water. In small rivers, currents are often swift and looking for shelter from the current becomes more of an issue for walleyes.

Just as you would while trout fishing, read the water for the best holding lies. There are some additional requirements that walleyes have for their holding water. The need for shade is still a driver, more so than with trout, and lies that provide shade are preferred. If deep water is available in the form of pools or if they can find undercut banks or weed beds, walleyes will use them to find shelter from the sun. In addition, river walleyes still eat mostly fish. Feeding lanes that channel drifting bugs to trout are not as much a need for walleyes as is ready access to pools and slack water where forage fish live.

I do most of my river fishing for walleye with subsurface flies. But remember that river walleyes see more insects than lake dwellers do, and for this reason, I think they're more likely to accept flies that embody the characteristics of both nymphs and fish. I use Woolly Buggers (white and black seem to be favorites) and marabous—backed up with Clousers and weighted Strip Minnows for working deep water.

Tackle and Gear for Walleyes

Walleyes require no special gear, so you may be able to use what you already own. The equipment I've suggested below would be a good choice if you're buying fly tackle just for walleye fishing.

Rods: Walleyes aren't particularly strong fish, nor are the flies you'll be casting to them really large. Six- or seven-weight tackle will be fine. Stream and river anglers may favor longer rods that will permit them to lob flies around pools without the necessity of making backcasts into overgrown banks.

Reels: Any solid single-action reel will be fine for walleyes, since the fish will place no unusual demands on your tackle.

Line: You already know my feelings about fishing really deep water with fly tackle. The bulk of my walleye fishing is done with floating lines and weighted flies. Sink-tip or even full-sink lines are worthy of consideration if you are patient and dedicated enough to wish to fish in the eight- to fifteen-foot depth range. As always, invest in a quality line.

There is a final line option that I mention with some reservations. You may decide that you want to fish deep—twenty feet deep and beyond—for walleyes, but you may also decide that a full-sink line is not for you. There is a cure, but it has a price. The cure is five feet to as much as twenty feet of lead-core trolling line that you connect to the end of your sink-tip line using loop-to-loop connections. This setup is available ready-made from a number of manufacturers. This line sinks, well, like lead, and by using this system it's possible to get your fly down deep in a hurry. The price you pay is that casting this affair is just awful, and doing so places quite a strain on your tackle. Gentle lob casts are the order of the day.

Clearly, such gear isn't for everybody, but if you absolutely demand the ability to plumb the depths in search of walleyes, a length of lead core is just the tool for the job.

Leaders: I use tapered bass leaders, averaging six- to eight-pound test, for most of my walleye fishing. Lighter trout leaders may not be up

Of all the fish in the book, the walleye probably requires the most in terms of "fishing smart," but flyfishing for them is very rewarding.

to being dragged across the rocky areas that walleyes frequent, and walleyes do have teeth that are hard on lighter leaders. I use long leaders (as much as twelve feet) when I'm fishing with a floating line, and short ones when I'm using sink-tip lines. As the fish go deeper, your leaders should get shorter. When I'm fishing for walleyes in what I consider to be deep water (ten to fifteen feet), I think a six-foot leader is a long one. Most of my deep leaders are about four feet in length.

Flies: Day in, day out, I catch most of my walleyes on Clouser Minnows in the colors I mentioned earlier in this chapter. My Clousers range from two to perhaps three-and-a-half inches in length, and by varying the size of the lead eyes, a variety of sink-rates and running depths can be achieved. Most of the Clousers I've seen are tied with bucktail, and I do use this material. Recently, however, I've been experimenting with synthetic hair, notably the crinkly, sparkly material. The added flash and translucency seems to interest walleyes more.

Other good walleye flies include Woolly Buggers (mostly in white and black), small Bunny Flies, Strip Minnows, and D's Minnows. Because I'm an eternal optimist, I always have a few big mayfly nymphs, emergers, and duns rattling around in my box.

Of all the fish in this book, the walleye probably requires the most in terms of "fishing smart": fishing for them when they are available and recognizing that there are times for the flyrodder when fishing for walleyes is a losing proposition. But fishing smart for walleyes is very rewarding. I take maximum advantage of the pre-spawn through post-spawn seasons and seek river-dwelling walleyes when the weather is hot. When I'm lucky enough to find myself on a dark, silent lake casting big mayflies to rising walleyes, it is, in many ways, the highlight of the year.

SEVEN

NORTHERN PIKE

I t's a sunny day in the early spring. You sit happily in your canoe, enjoying the feel of the sun on your back and the four-weight in your hand as you cast little poppers into a patch of lily pads. You're picking up sunfish pretty regularly, and all in all, the world is a pretty good place. You cast, your popper lands with a discreet "plunk," and a moment later a bluegill obligingly makes it disappear. You play the little fish carefully, enjoying the tussle.

Then things begin to go haywire. From the shallows a torpedo-like shape suddenly charges out at the frantic bluegill. There's a flash of white as jaws engulf the hapless bluegill, a moment of frightening stress on your light tackle. Then, without warning, the line goes slack. In an instant, the bluegill, your fly, the tippet, and that big, fast, deadly fish have all vanished as if they never existed. You find that your hands are shaking, you're holding your breath, and you're staring blankly at the water.

Congratulations, you've had about as polite an introduction to northern pike as you're likely to get.

Some years ago, I read a story in a magazine about pike. Little knowing what I was getting into, I visited a local lake with spinning tackle. On occasion, fortune favors the novice, and on that first day of

The first time three-and-a-half feet and over twenty pounds of fish charges your fly, you're likely to walk down the road to pike fishing madness.

my pike fishing I caught a forty-five inch, twenty-five pound monster. I became an immediate convert to pike fishing, and since I was already flyfishing for trout, I began toying with the idea of fishing for pike with fly tackle. From toying with the idea, I moved to experimentation. When the experiments were successful, I became a walking, talking pike fanatic.

At first any pike taken on fly tackle excited me. But later the search for large pike became a consuming passion. I say this to give you fair warning! The first time three-and-a-half feet and over twenty pounds of fish charges your fly, the first time the water literally explodes as a pike savages your popper, you are very likely to walk down the same road to pike fishing madness that I've traveled.

Northern Pike Habits and Habitat

To scientists the northern pike is known as *Esox lucius* (water wolf), but like any thug it travels under a variety of aliases: snake, 'gator, great northern pike, and blue pike, among others.

Pike are distributed worldwide, and the largest pike of all live in Europe where they frequent brackish water and, perhaps, in some of the near-virgin lakes in Siberia. Pike are a relative newcomer to our shores, probably migrating through brackish waters from Siberia along the Bering Strait into North America millions of years ago. They've done well here, and they now probably represent your best odds of catching a fish of over twenty pounds in freshwater.

Pike prefer cool waters, and though small, stunted populations of pike do manage to survive in the southern part of the United States, pike thrive in the northern part of the country and in Canada, partic- ularly in prairie states and provinces where altitudes or latitudes are sufficient to provide the cool waters pike prefer.

Pike are a long, lean fish. In general their backs range in color through shades of green and brown, marked by rows of lighter, bean- shaped spots. Their bellies are cream or light yellow through pure white, and their fins range from greenish gold and brown to pure red. Many color variations exist, and pure silver, barred, and spotted pike also occur.

The long, lean body shape and the concentration of caudal, dor- sal, and anal fins at the rear of the fish all suggest speed, and in fact a pike may approach twenty miles per hour during its initial mad rush in full pursuit of prey. But pike are really sprinters, hunters from ambush, and they're not capable of sustaining the speed that their body shape suggests they could.

While possessing excellent lateral line sense, pike are primarily sight-feeders, and a pike's eyes are placed high and to the rear of the head, much like the alligator it's sometimes named for. While this gives the pike excellent ability to search for prey, it also results in blind spots directly in front of the fish and below the head.

Pike can grow rapidly (over a foot in the first year of life in mild climates, perhaps six inches in cold areas), and this rapid growth rate is sustained by a voracious appetite. A pike can eat a fish one-third its size without strain, and a large pike will dine happily on such diverse items as fish, frogs, ducks, and muskrats. I've often caught pike with part of their last meal still protruding from their gullets, and more than once, I've found the bodies of pike that miscalculated and literally choked to death on a large fish that wouldn't quite fit down their throats. Keep

The northern's long, lean body shape and concentration of fins at the rear suggest speed, but a pike is a sprinter, a hunter from ambush.

in mind that northern pike are as opportunistic as any other predator, and while I wouldn't recommend fishing for northerns with nymph patterns, I've also taken pike that were literally full to the gills with a cargo of damselfly nymphs.

Seasons of the Northern Pike

The pike's combination of appetite and sheer aggressiveness is good news to the flyrodder; those traits combine to produce a fish that is a willing taker of large flies. Even better, pike spend significant periods of time in shallow water (in fact, in northern climes, they may spend all year in the shallows), making them very accessible to the flyrodder. Let's follow northerns through the seasons to see when they're most available to the flyfisher.

Pre-spawn Northerns

Pre-spawn conditions for pike begin at the time ice leaves the lake until spawning commences at water temperatures of thirty-nine to forty-five degrees. At the lower end of this range, pike begin moving toward the shallows from the deeper waters where they spent the winter, and they will stage at the first drop-off awaiting consistently warmer temperatures. The males arrive first to be joined by the much larger gravid females a few days or a week later. Male pike are significantly smaller than the females; it's rare that a male exceeds thirty inches in length.

Shallow, dark-bottomed, back-bay areas warm first and consequently attract pike earlier than other parts of the lake. Small feeder creeks that pump warm water into lakes can also attract pike. Pike prefer to spawn in cover when it's available, so they also seek weed growth, both emergent aquatic vegetation and flooded terrestrial weeds and brush.

At this time both sexes are together in significant numbers, are aggressive, and are feeding to support the spawn, during which they will stop eating. As waters continue to warm, pike spend more time in the shallows, particularly during the heat of the day. Although the fish are feeding, water temperatures are still on the cool side, and the pike are more sluggish than they would normally be.

Because pike become active so early in the year, you may miss pre-spawn altogether. In fact, in some northern lakes, pike are known to spawn under the ice. But if you're able to fish for pre-spawn pike, there are a few considerations you should keep in mind in addition to the ones I've mentioned. For instance, this is the first time during the year when pike concentrate in significant numbers. You may only see one or two of the impeccably camouflaged pike, but almost certainly, more are present. Retrieves should be slow; I use twelve-inch strips at this time of the year.

To maximize your odds of success when temperatures are toward the lower end of the pre-spawn range, fish during the hottest portion of the day. And keep an eye on the wind direction. As I discussed in the first chapter, the surface of the lake warms first, and wind pushes this warmer surface water to the downwind side of the lake. The ideal pre-spawn pike flyfishing situation might be summarized as arriving at a dark-bottomed bay on the downwind side of a lake at about 1:00 P.M. on a warm day and fishing areas where vegetation is just starting to emerge adjacent to the first drop-off.

Cool days, clouds, or a cool spring rain all keep temperatures low, and the pike will sulk in their drop-off staging areas. However, as temperatures warm, the pike will be able to spend more time in the shallows and will finally move in to spawn.

Spawning Northerns

When water temperatures stay consistently in the forty to fifty degree range, pike get down to the serious business of spawning. The males and females are both in the shallows now, and the fish are seeking weedy areas in which to lay their eggs. These areas range in depth from literally inches of water to as much as three feet of water.

For pike, the ideal nursery has a dark bottom, which warms faster than the surrounding lake. It may be further enhanced by a small feeder creek that pumps warm water into the lake. Emergent vegetation provides cover for the spawning fish, their eggs, and newly hatched pike fry. Conditions sometimes force pike to spawn in less than ideal circumstances, of course.

The spawning act is a vigorous one, accompanied by much splashing and thrashing on the part of the males, which may help to distribute the eggs. Unlike the members of the bass family, pike are not a nesting fish, and after the eggs are laid, they're abandoned. Spawning may last for two to three weeks. After the females spawn, they retreat to deeper water for a week or so to recuperate. The males remain in the shallows, and when the females rejoin them, the very productive post-spawn season is at hand. Locating spawning bays is very important, because they're the key, along with water temperature and food availability, to the best pike fishing of the year, the post-spawn season.

Throughout this book, I've urged you to give spawning fish a break, to let them get the vital reproductive act done in peace. I urge you to do the same for pike, but not just because the spawn is important. Pike aren't active feeders during the spawn and fishing for spawning pike is just not very productive. While the pike are spawning, it's time pursue other quarry.

Post-spawn Northerns

Post-spawn flyfishing for pike is some of the best action available to the flyrodder who is making the journey beyond trout. Both sexes are working the shallows (the big females are back!), the pike are once again present in significant numbers, and they are feeding heavily on minnows, young-of-the-year (mom and dad, for that matter), and anything else they can fit their jaws around. Post-spawn water temperatures range from fifty-eight to sixty-eight degrees.

Pike remain in the shallows until warming waters drive them deeper. In some lakes, post-spawn pike may be in the shallows for several weeks; in others, they may remain for well over a month. In those wonderful lakes in the Far North, pike may remain in the shallows all summer long. Food is another important determinant of when (or if) pike leave the shallows. In lakes where available forage fish such as sunfish prefer the shallows, pike will stay in the shallows even if they have to accept warmer temperatures than they like. In other lakes, forage fish such as ciscoes may range considerably deeper, and pike leave the shallows to pursue them as water temperatures increase.

To find large numbers of pike that are feeding aggressively, don't miss the post-spawn season, no matter where you fish. Post-spawn pike are feeding in shallow water, and they're hungry. If you miss the opportunity to throw floating flies to these fish, you've missed the most fun you're likely to have during the season. Often several fish will charge your fly, and the strikes are very, very violent. Because the fish are in the shallows, you'll frequently cast to fish you can see, and the ferocious plunge of one or more fish for your fly will be visible from start to finish. The fish are often tightly grouped at this time, so if you catch one, cast again! One of the pike that missed out the last time may be quicker on the trigger the second time around.

Even very large pike can be found in water only six to eight inches deep during the post-spawn.

Post-spawn pike are most active during the daylight hours, and I try to be casting to them from 11:00 A.M. to about 6:00 P.M. While many pike may return to their spawning areas, water temperatures and the availability of forage can drive them elsewhere, and you'll have to go pike hunting. Take water temperatures and look for areas that provide food and cover for the pike's prey: sunfish, young bass, and minnows. Shallow areas with thick weed growth and other cover that supports good insect and crustacean populations are good places to hunt pike. At the lower end of the post-spawn temperature range, the shallow water you're searching may be only six to eight inches in depth. Even very large pike can be found in water this shallow. When and if water temperatures move into the higher end of the post-spawn range, the pike will gradually move into deeper water.

Remember that pike prefer to hunt from ambush. Areas of thick weed growth, deadfall, and undercut banks all provide shadowed cover that permits pike to virtually disappear. Cast to these areas even if you don't see pike—you'll often be pleasantly surprised. All the time you're pike fishing, you'll be doing your best to spot pike, something that requires practice.

All the time you're fishing, you'll be doing your best to spot the impeccably camouflaged pike. Pike can virtually disappear in weeds and deadfall.

Retrieves and fly selection during the post-spawn are a matter of experimentation. It's a time to vary your retrieves. You may find that the slow, bouncing, almost jig-like retrieve of a subsurface fly works best. Other times small twitches of a popper or diver will provoke strikes. Still other times, you will find yourself making a big Bunny Fly literally zip through the water with three-foot monster strips.

There's a frustrating pike behavior that can happen any time of the year. It's known as the follow, and there are two kinds. The most common one occurs when a pike settles in a few inches behind your fly, follows it virtually back to your feet, and then quietly swims away. After this happens for the fourth or fifth time, you'll be reduced to a state of near insanity. I suspect that the explanation for this kind of follow has to do with the pike's blind spot. When a pike gets quite close to your fly, it may simply lose sight of it. This is particularly apt to happen in shallow water, where the pike's cone of vision is reduced. Now, a real baitfish would never let a pike get that close for long. It would flee erratically and pass out of the blind spot to where the pike could track it again. Your fly should do the same: speed your retrieve and move the fly to one side or the other, where the pike has better vision.

In the second kind of follow, the pike may give up on your fly quite early in the game. While I make no claims to being able to read a pike's mind, what I think has happened is that your fly isn't traveling fast enough to convince the pike that it's prey. Once again, a faster and perhaps more erratic retrieve may provide the solution.

Summer Northerns

In pike fishing, summer occurs if and when the water in the shallows warms to the point that the pike are driven into deep water. On their journey to cooler water, the pike will, if they can, travel on aquatic highways in the form of old creek channels, gullies, or other structure that provides cover. If you can find these features, they're excellent areas to work as pike move out of the shallows when the temperatures warm and back into the shallows in the cool of the morning or evening and during cool, cloudy days.

These movements usually commence when water temperatures are above seventy degrees. In warmer parts of the country, water temperatures may stay high for several months. This sounds like bad news for the flyfisher, but don't despair! Pike usually don't move beyond the ultimate reach of the flyfisher; often they're found near the first drop-off in

Summer pike usually don't move beyond the reach of the flyfisher. Brad Befus

eight to perhaps twelve feet of water, where they have access to the shallows and can move in to feed.

That puts them in relatively deep water for the flyfisher, and in preceding chapters of this book, I've explained that I don't like to fish deep water with fly tackle. I make an exception when it comes to pike. What makes pike so different? I suppose the decision to fish deep depends on what sort of angler you are. While I personally am reluctant to work deep water for a one-pound fish such as crappie, I do find it very exciting to fish deep water when my potential return is a twenty-pound or larger fish.

This is also a time when the young-of-the-year and small baitfish move farther afield in search of their food. The pike follow them, and the end result is that although they are still feeding consistently and may remain in water shallow enough to fish, pike are scattered.

While pike may spend time at the first drop-off adjacent to a post-spawn feeding area, there are other locations that can also draw pike. If you can find them, springs provide a source of cool water, and pike will hold near them, particularly if there is some cover available. Stream inlets may also provide cooler waters and permit pike to stay in the shallows. Finally, in areas where the water temperature is nearly right, something as simple as a shadow may cool the water enough for pike. The shade provided by tall trees and the shadows cast by an island or even an overhanging bank may all hold pike.

Regardless of where they elect to wait out the dog days, pike still seek cover. Don't ignore the edges of weedlines or submerged timber or brush. It's also important to remember that shallow hunting areas are not necessarily along the shoreline. Islands, saddle areas with shallow, weedy growth, and old creek channels (all of which may offer rapid access to deep, cool water) are excellent places to cast a fly at this time of year if you have a belly boat or canoe.

Even a pike fanatic has to admit that pike can move beyond the reach of fly tackle. There are two things you can do at this point. First, you can move back into the shallows after the bass and bluegills that will now be active. Or, you can try fishing for pike in rivers. I'll talk about that in just a moment.

Fall Northerns

As water temperatures drop into the sixties, pike will spend more time in shallow water, and I like to think of this as the beginning of the fall pike season. As was the case with spring fishing, this move is a gradual one, and at the start of fall, pike spend most of the day in their summer locations. Then as temperatures continue to drop, they'll spend more and more time in the shallows. These fish are still scattered, and it's worth emphasizing again that shallow water does not necessarily mean a return to the spawning bays. The vegetation in the shallows is beginning to die off, insect hatches are slowing, and minnows and the young-of-the-year have scattered. Pike respond to these changes in their environment by seeking shallow water in saddle areas around islands, rock reefs, and points with deep water access, all areas where you can cast to them efficiently.

Turnover occurs at this time of the year, further scattering fish throughout the lake. In some areas, turnover is followed fairly quickly by the advent of ice on the lake. In such a case, the lake doesn't have time to restratify, and your odds of catching pike after turnover are slim. In other areas, several weeks or a month may pass before the lake finally freezes, allowing the lake to restratify to some extent. In those lakes, pike may return to the shallows on a warm day, when the water temperature in a back bay may rise to forty-five degrees or so. By the time water temperatures are consistently in the low forties, pike action has come to a virtual halt for the flyfisher.

Fall pike tactics are determined by what is happening around you. If spring is a time of beginnings, fall is a time of endings. Weed growth in shallow spawning areas is dying or moving into a dormant state. Baitfish and minnows that survived the summer have grown substantially. And pike, facing a long winter under the ice and the need to produce next spring's supply of milt and eggs, are feeding heavily.

Fall is big pike time, and these fish are looking for big meals in the form of the large minnows and baitfish that avoided becoming lunch earlier in the year. While all pike flies are large, I routinely fish with six- to seven-inch flies in the fall. I fish the saddles, reefs, creek channels, and points mentioned above, and I keep an eye on the thermometer.

At the higher end of the fall temperature range, the fish are essentially in a summer pattern: they are reasonably likely to come up for a surface fly, and overall they are active. Fast retrieves, big flies, and the ability to fish both surface and subsurface flies are important considerations. As water temperatures continue to drop, pike become more sluggish, just as they were in early spring. That is the time to begin slowing your retrieves, moving back to the twelve-inch strips that you used in the spring, and to concentrate more on putting the fly where the fish are. Large, comparatively slow-moving subsurface patterns become more important.

If you were to graph what's happening at this time of year, I think you would end up with a classic bell-shaped curve: poor feeding at the higher end of the fall temperature range, when waters are a bit too warm, moving to an increase in feeding as temperatures fall through the sixties and high fifties, followed by another decrease in feeding as water temperatures drop into the low fifties and the forties.

Fall is a big pike time, and these fish are looking for big meals.

River Northerns

For the true pike fanatic, rivers are a fine place to flyfish for pike during the heat of the summer—or any other time—because rivers are often both cooler and shallower than lakes. Pike can inhabit rivers successfully if there isn't too much current or if there's sufficient cover present to shelter them from the current.

In large, slow rivers, the pike behave essentially as though they lived in a long, narrow lake, and they can be found in typical lake-like locations. In faster rivers (pike can even coexist with trout), the current becomes an issue. In these rivers, the trout fishers in the audience will feel right at home. Since pike can't hang effortlessly in a run or riffle the way trout can, they must seek shelter from the current, and they must have access to lots of food. The substantial difference between trout and pike in a river is that the pike need *more*: more shelter from the current and access to more or bigger food items.

But pike have something going for them—they're really tough customers, and they're capable of securing the best areas for themselves. The pike's need for more in the way of cover and food, and its ability to secure places that offer both, determine river pike tactics.

Spawning in rivers will occur at roughly the same times and water temperatures as in lakes. In the spring of the year, runoff may place the river at its highest and fastest, resulting in flooding, and pike happily spawn in areas of flooded terrestrial vegetation and brush. Because the banks of rivers are often heavily overgrown, this can result in the need to fish in very heavy brush. Weed guards, heavy leaders, and strong language may all apply.

After the spawn, pike seek lies just as trout do—but they get the very best of them. My recommendation for river pike fishers is to look at the available lies and cast your pike flies to the biggest and best of them. A big rock, a large stretch of flat water, the outside edge of a big, slow bend, and large logs or areas of deadfall can all provide the premium cover that pike prefer. Deep pools, which provide shelter from the current for food fish, are also prime pike locations.

Finally, although pike are never a genuinely social fish, the limited number of good pike lies may force them to live together. If you snooker one pike from a lie, cast again, but move a bit farther into the lie. A larger pike, which has been able to reserve the very best part of the lie for itself, may be present.

Tackle and Gear for Northerns

Flyfishing for pike requires special consideration of the tackle you'll be using. The need to throw big, heavy flies determines in large part the tackle a pike flyfisher uses.

Rods: Although pike aren't as strong as saltwater fish of the same size and weight, I fish for pike with saltwater-sized gear. Nine- and ten-

Big flies are required for big northerns. Saltwater-sized gear is needed to cast flies the size of a small brookie.

weight, nine- and ten-foot rods are the standard for me, not because of the size and strength of the fish, but because of the BIG flies I cast. Lighter tackle simply isn't up to casting flies the size of a small brookie.

Reels: Heavier lines and bigger rods mean bigger reels, and you'll have some decisions to make. The pike rods I use are also designed for saltwater use, and because I fish saltwater fairly regularly, I purchase high-quality saltwater reels. However, reels of this caliber often carry frightening price tags. You may decide to start out with a good single-action freshwater reel and, if and when you're ready for a trip to Christmas Island, invest in a saltwater reel later.

Lines: Weight-forward floating and sink-tip lines will handle the bulk of your pike fishing needs. In fact, I probably use a floating line ninety percent of the time. I don't recommend lines designed for saltwater flyfishing, because they're made to be used in hot weather and can become cranky in cool-water applications. Recently, a couple of manufacturers have introduced lines developed just for pike fishing, with finishes that will take a beating from the cover that pike love so well. I use these lines and I've found them to be excellent.

Leaders: For many years, pike flyfishers used only heavy monofilament leaders tipped with wire shock tippets. They work well and are a particularly good choice when fishing in heavy cover, because the small-diameter wire shock tippet can slice through cabbage and the like. A simpler solution (and the one I use) is to fish with hard-monofilament level leaders. I've found that they work very well for pike fishing, as long as the leader is religiously checked for nicks by passing it between your lips. The leaders I use range from twenty-five to thirty-pound test and nine- to ten-foot lengths.

Climax recently introduced a leader material made from a woven tungsten and steel formulation. This thin, supple, terrifically strong material promises to be the leader of choice for pike and other toothy game fish.

Flies: Pike flies are BIG. My favorite, all-time best pike producer is the Bunny Fly (tied with rabbit strips in the style of a giant Woolly Bugger) in white, black, chartreuse, yellow, orange, and various color combinations. The bulk of my Bunny Flies are tied on size 3/0 hooks, and they range from four to seven inches in length. Because pike *bite* flies, durability is an issue, and Bunny Flies stand up well. Other good choices for subsurface work include large D's Minnows (baby rainbow, baitfish, and bluegill) and Strip Minnows (imitating the same species). These flies also offer excellent durability.

For anglers who are starting out with lighter tackle, say a six-weight outfit, the Barr 'Bou Face provides a large silhouette, ample motion in the water, and the ease of casting a smaller, lighter fly. Although they're not as durable as "leather" pike flies, they will permit you to fish for subsurface pike without investing in new gear. Other good choices include Whistlers, Lefty's Deceivers (white, olive, and baitfish colors), and large conventional streamer patterns. The caveat is that not only do pike chew the heck out of flies, they also drag them through weeds and brush. Durability will suffer.

For surface work, size 2/0 and 3/0 poppers and slider patterns are effective. Although hair patterns may be easier to cast for users of light tackle, pike can quickly turn tough-to-tie, expensive hair poppers into scrap. Cork is a better choice, and the new foam-headed popper patterns, which are nearly as light as deer-hair poppers, are probably the best choice of all. I have found that white, black, purple, chartreuse, yellow, and orange are all good producers.

Divers permit you to eat your cake and have it, too, since they create a commotion on the surface but can also be used for shallow subsurface work. Coupled with sink-tip or full-sink lines, they can be made to dive several feet deep, thereby allowing the angler to prospect a significant slice of water. Using a giant megadiver-style fly is a particularly good way to catch the attention of a pike by presenting your quarry

When a northern rips your popper off the surface and tries to beat up you and your tackle, the trip to pike fishing madness may not seem so bad. Bryce Snellgrove

with a large, meaty looking silhouette. Black and white are my first choices, although purple, chartreuse, yellow, and orange have produced well for me.

The bulk of my pike flies are tied on size 2/0 and 3/0 hooks, and subsurface or surface, I rarely tie anything less than four inches long or more than seven inches long.

I gave you a warning at the beginning of this chapter: just one pike on a fly rod may be enough to send you down the road to pike-fishing madness. I hope what I've told you about my favorite beyond-trout fish leaves you feeling that the trip may not be so bad. I know you'll feel that way the first time a northern rips your popper off the surface and tries its best to beat up you and your tackle. See you on down the road.

EIGHT

TIGER MUSKIE

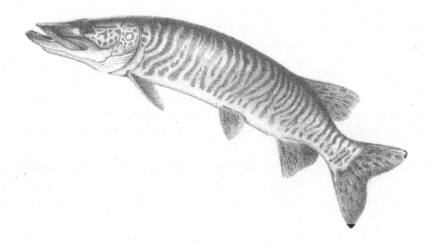

Fisheries managers probably have as many impossible dreams as the rest of us. I suspect that, until tiger muskies became popular, many of their dreams ran to fantasies of a fast growing, adaptable, top-level predator fish that could be used to control rough fish. They might also have hoped that the fish would have flashy looks, fighting and leaping ability, and be a challenge to catch, making it a favorite of anglers. Finally, if they dreamed long enough, the fish would be a predator whose population could somehow be controlled so that they wouldn't awaken one dark morning to discover all their other game fish missing.

Dreams do come true, because the tiger muskie is exactly that sort of fish. The tiger muskie is a sterile hybrid, a cross between the northern pike (*Esox lucius*) and the muskellunge (*Esox masquinongy*), which gives it, in the best tradition of inbred aristocracy, both a true double-barreled name (*Esox lucius* x *Esox masquinongy*) and nonexistent reproductive success.

Its sterility makes the tiger a popular fish among fisheries managers, but not just because they can be sure that tiger populations won't explode. For many fish, spawning is the most energy-intensive thing they do, and the need to spawn limits growth and contributes to natural mortality among mature fish. Because the tiger doesn't spawn, it can use that energy for growth. Tigers can reach forty inches in length in only five or six years.

Tigers are more distinctly colored than their parents, resembling the silver and vertically barred phase of certain true muskies. In tigers the barring is more vivid and uniform. Although they don't exhibit the wide color variations common to their parents, other tiger color forms do exist, among them pure silver.

The tiger has also carved out a place in the hearts of anglers. With its striking markings, the tiger is the showman of the pike clan. Tigers fight just as hard as any northern or true muskie, and they are born acrobats, as well. The sight of a dramatically marked fish over three feet long taking to the air—repeatedly—is a scene that will etch itself in the memory of any angler.

My first tiger had wings. I was fishing a local lake that had been stocked with tigers to control perch and rough fish populations. It was in the early summer, and I was fishing to shallow tigers that I could spot easily. Knowing nothing to the contrary, I was using pike tactics and although I had repeated follows, I failed to hook up. This lack of success made me careless, and when the fifth or sixth large tiger of the day started trailing my fly, I paid little attention. The fish got to within perhaps twelve feet of me when, with a sudden flick of its tail, it inhaled the fly.

Startled, I set the hook, ready for the fish to run. Instead, it instantly left the water, actually splashing me in the process. To say I was shocked would be a gross understatement—I was totally unprepared. If I hadn't had a good hook set, I would have lost the fish. If anything, I was even more surprised when the tiger continued to jump, alternating its leaps with vigorous runs. In the time it took me to land the fish, I arrived at a firm decision: I'd be doing a lot more tiger fishing.

Tiger Muskie Habits and Habitat

Although a tiger looks a lot like a pike, it's worth emphasizing something right away: a tiger is *not* a brightly colored, dressed-up northern pike. Nor is it exactly a true muskie, either. A tiger is a very different fish, one that requires different tactics than either of its parents.

A northern will often charge a fly the moment it hits the water, but a tiger is more likely to swim for a long distance with its nose right behind the fly, coming almost to the angler's feet, only to swim away, leaving the angler, with pumping heart and shaking knees, to make pointed comments about the fish's mixed ancestry.

A tiger muskie is not a brightly colored, dressed-up northern pike. Nor is it a true muskie. A tiger is a very different fish requiring special tactics.

In the chapter on northern pike, I mentioned that I've often caught northerns that had their last dinner still protruding from their gullet and that, on other occasions, I'd found northerns that had literally choked to death on a fish that was too big for them to swallow. This seems indicative of a fish that often strikes a fly from sheer bad temper, aggressiveness, or instinct, rather than purely from hunger. That doesn't seem to be the case with tigers.

When the tigers stocked in Colorado first attained trophy status, I made a practice of calling local taxidermists to inquire what the trophy tigers that came into their shops had in their bellies. Their answers were uniform: the bellies were empty. Are tigers less aggressive and therefore more likely to strike out of hunger? Are they more selective than northerns? Or because they don't spawn and overrun the lakes in which they live, do they face less competitive pressure within their predatory niche, and can they therefore be more blasé about opportunities to feed?

I don't know. Whatever the reason (and I suspect that it may be a combination of all of the above reasons), tigers are simply more challenging to catch than northerns. They're less likely to take the first casually presented fly they see, more likely to follow a fly and examine it carefully, and more likely to demand realistic offerings.

Tigers prefer warmer waters than do northerns, which makes them suitable for stocking in more areas of the United States. They are also more likely to be loners than are northerns and, except in the spring, are rarely found together in significant numbers. In this respect they are more like the muskie side of the family than the northern. Like both of its parents, the tiger is predominantly a sight feeder, although it also possesses the sensitive lateral line common to all pike.

It's worth mentioning two other rather perplexing behaviors common to the fish. Tigers will often swim on the surface, with their heads completely out of the water, for extended periods of time. Although some of my friends jokingly say that the tigers are hunting belly boaters, I've never heard a really good explanation for this behavior.

The second characteristic involves porpoising, repeated surfacing and submerging. This behavior can occur seemingly without cause, but it's also often linked to being released or to the fish being spooked. Often, when the tiger finally submerges, it trails a stream of bubbles, leading me to guess that the behavior has something to do with the fish seeking to maintain pressure levels in its swim bladder, but this is simply a wild guess on my part.

Speaking of spooked, when you spook a tiger (and you will), while you're muttering an expletive or two, carefully make a note of the spot the tiger came from. Tigers are homebodies, and if you rest the fish for a half-hour or so, you can often return (more carefully this time) to find the tiger back in its old haunts.

Seasons of the Tiger Muskie

Throughout this book, many of the movements of the fish I've discussed are driven by the need to feed for the spawn, to spawn, and to recover from the spawning act. It's only fitting that there should be an exception to the rule, and the tiger is such an exception, since it doesn't spawn. However, tigers still make many of the same seasonal movements common to other fish species, and by knowing where and when to fish, you can hunt tigers much more successfully.

Spring Tigers

There is no pre-spawn in the sense that I've described it elsewhere in this book, but like other fish, the movement of tigers is determined by water temperature and food availability.

It's true that tigers move into the shallows in the spring, and it's true that they seek out the dark-bottomed bays that warm earliest. It's also true that at this time of the year they're found together in greater numbers than at other times of the year. And most significantly, they move into the shallows early in the year—before water temperatures warm sufficiently to permit them to feed heavily. All in all, it appears that the fish are moving in response to a residual urge to spawn. But is there a false spawn? Perhaps. Perhaps not.

Let's bear in mind that the shallows come to life first. Couldn't the tigers be responding to warming waters, coming in to await other fish that will also move in to spawn? I've never seen any pairing off of tigers, nor have I ever observed the splashy fandangos that characterize courtship and spawning among pike. I think the jury is still out on this issue, and for the angler, the important thing to recognize is that tigers, although they're not spawning, do make the same sort of move to the shallows that their fertile parents do.

At ice-out, when water temperatures are still below forty, tigers are usually holding in deep water. Unlike the "cooler" pike, tigers remain sluggish at this temperature range. When water temperatures range from forty-five to fifty, their movement into the shallows begins.

At the lower end of this temperature range, tigers begin to gather at the first drop-off. As the water temperatures rise toward fifty, tigers begin to move into back-bay areas. As you might expect, darker bottoms and bays with large expanses of shallows are preferred. They seek cover, just as spawning northerns do, and they can be found on the inside and outside edges of emerging weedlines, near deadfall, and around other structures that conceal and protect them. Again like northerns, tigers will take advantage of warm feeder creeks and will use highways in the form of submerged creek channels or other structure on their way into the shallows.

By the time water temperatures have risen into the fifties, tigers spend much more time in the shallows, but as I observed above, they're not feeding heavily. This is a frustrating time for the angler, because you can see large numbers of fish, but casting to them is often disappointing. This period lasts for one or two weeks, suspiciously like the reduction in feeding that occurs during the spawn of true pike. Tactically, this is a good time to fish for crappie, walleyes, and northern pike.

The good news is that this slow time doesn't last all that long, and when water temperatures reach the mid-fifties to low sixties, tigers become active, resulting in one of the better fishing times of the year. The bad news is that the fish scatter fairly quickly, leaving the bays in search of food.

The brief period in spring when waters have warmed enough to encourage feeding but before tigers scatter is your best chance to catch one on the fly.

This brief period of time, when the waters have warmed enough to encourage feeding but before the fish scatter, is perhaps your best chance to catch a hungry tiger that may let its belly overcome its better judgment. Since this is the first really active feed of the year, tigers are hungry and less selective than they are later in the season (but still more selective than true pike).

Like all members of the pike family, tigers are ambushers, and finding them is to some extent a matter of finding areas where food is present and where tigers have good lurking spots. Areas of newly emergent weed growth, particularly along the first drop-off, are worth thorough coverage through the use of systematic fan-casting. Areas of downed timber can also provide cover for baitfish and the tigers that seek them. But don't ignore the shallows! They are fish factories at this time of year, and tigers, particularly in the morning and evening, cruise in shallow water, preying on young baitfish and minnows. Careful study of a map can often provide you with the location of old creek channels or other topographic features that serve to channel the tigers' movements into and out of the shallows.

I've caught most of my tigers on subsurface flies. While a northern will belt a popper or diver out of what may be sheer savagery, a tiger seems to prefer to chase something that more closely resembles dinner. In spring, dinner is small in comparison to meals taken during the rest of the year, and I cast smaller flies than I do at any other time—three-and-a-half to four-and-a-half inches is about average.

Unlike pike, which will happily grab a chartreuse and hot-pink horror that bears no relation to anything that swims, tigers always seem to show a decided preference for flies that offer a resemblance to forage fish. Larger baitfish patterns tied to match the local forage are in order.

The real key is matching the food that is most abundant yet still offers a good energy return. While the lake in spring may swarm with millions of eighth-inch fry of a variety of species, three-and-a-half-inch spottails may be what the tigers are actually eating. Later they may pass on the spottails because meatier prey in the form of six-inch bluegills is available to them.

Summer Tigers

Tigers are in their summer behavior pattern when water temperatures range from sixty-five to about seventy-five degrees. It's the period of peak activity for tigers, but it's not necessarily the angler's best time.

Earlier in the season, tigers were hungry, and the forage base was at a low. This time of year, just the opposite is true. Young fish are at their most numerous and they're growing rapidly. Larger baitfish and game fish have spawned, becoming more active, and therefore better targets for tigers. All in all, tigers can afford to be more selective than at any other time of the year.

All anglers are lucky at one time or another, but I think good anglers make their own luck. One way to do this is to spend time on the water, systematically showing up at the right places at the right times. I've developed a system that works for me at all times of the year, and I think that by following these guidelines your tiger hunting will be more successful, not only in summer, but year around.

Step 1. Set up a route. More than learning a lake well and understanding where tigers live, this means visiting those places every time you fish the lake. This is important because, as we've seen, tigers are most likely to strike flies when their bellies are empty. You may visit a tiger many times over the course of the season—and the more often you visit, the more likely you are to find it when it's ready for a meal.

Step 2. Fish the productive times of the day. Traveling in circles around a lake for six or eight hours in pursuit of sluggish fish is a sure ticket to madness. In the summer, maximize your odds of success by hunting tigers early in the morning and late in the evening. Take the afternoon off and go catch a few bass.

Step 3. Fish bigger flies. While northerns may snap at a size 8 Woolly Bugger just for the hell of it, tigers seem to be looking for food. Size 2/0 and 3/0 flies are my standards in the summer, and they range from five to seven inches long. Imitations of local baitfish, such as shiners, chubs, and baby bass, seem to be more effective than impressionistic offerings.

Step 4. Fish to as many fish as you can. This is a deceptively simple statement, so stop giggling! All fishing is to some extent a numbers game, and within limits, the fellow who casts the most, catches the most. And what are those limits? You have to cast where the fish are and you have to be casting to them when they're hungry.

Step 5. Concentrate on areas known to be productive at the time of the year you're fishing. Willie Sutton robbed banks because, "That's where they keep all the money." Willie had a point. In the summer, search the inside and outside edges of weedlines, creek channels, downed timber, riprap along dams, saddle areas, rock reefs, and islands. Keep in mind that deep-water access is viewed as a plus by tigers, both for the cooler temperatures available and for additional protection from predators.

In summer, fish "where they keep all the tigers," weedlines, creek channels, and downed timber.

They also need cover, both for protection and to conceal them from prey. Tigers also have to eat, so access to shallow hunting areas or structure that attracts forage fish is sought out.

You will be looking for tigers, trying to spot them visually. Like all pike, tigers are masters of camouflage, and spotting them will be difficult. Wear polarized sunglasses to help you see the fish (if you don't wear eye protection when you fish, you should) and back up your shades with a wide-brimmed hat.

Step 6. Make your line system work for you. I use sink-tip lines for most of my summer tiger hunting. Every moment you spend waiting for your fly to sink is a moment spent not fishing for tigers, and over the course of a day, those moments amount to a considerable amount of time. A sink-tip line puts your fly where it needs to be faster, keeps your fly running at productive depths longer, and does much to maximize your odds of success.

The summer of my first year of tiger hunting was miserable. My favorite tiger lake is gin-clear, and I could see the fish when I ran my route—long, dark shadows hanging motionless, sometimes near deep cover, sometimes on the bottom itself. My flies never reached them, and consequently I never caught them. Finally I wised up and began using a sink-tip line. It's a matter of getting a fish that has found good cover, that may find the water a bit warm, and that has probably been feeding regularly to leave its shady den and pursue your fly. This means placing a nice, fat meal right in front of its snout, and for this task, a sink-tip line is ideal.

From a seasonal perspective, flexibility is really the key. Early and late summer can provide periods of surface action for tigers, and in early spring you may want to slip a subsurface fly just under the film in the shallows. Take a minute or so to change lines, rather than trying to get by with an inappropriate line choice.

Step 7. Be persistent. Travel your route more than once. This is another one of those deceptively simple statements. Persistence means more than covering a prospective area thoroughly—it also means taking advantage of the tiger. In the summer, for example, early in the morning, when you first come calling, Mr. Tiger has just spent a long, cool night at home. It may be a bit sluggish. But if you come back later that morning or that evening, it's had some time to bask in the sun. Its metabolism is up, it's burned a few calories, and it might be thinking about a snack.

This sort of approach requires discipline and it can become monotonous at times. On the other hand, I find that a thirty-pound fish jumping right in my face is *never* monotonous . . . so I pay my dues.

Fall Tigers

Fall for the tiger marks a time when water temperatures move down from the sixties. The fish are located in the same areas as in summer, but as temperatures fall, tigers move into deeper water, returning to the shallows to forage during the heat of the day. As water temperatures continue to drop, the fish spend more of each day in deep water, and by the time water temperatures reach the mid-forties, tiger hunting season is about over for the year.

The tigers' movement into deeper water can be due to factors other than falling temperatures. In one of my favorite lakes, tigers move into deep water along with large schools of perch, far beyond the reach of fly tackle. I often spot these fish on a fish-finder, shown as huge arches suspended over smaller arches that represent the perch. Sometimes I wave at them . . . sometimes I make another gesture entirely.

This is the time to refine both your route and your timing. In the morning and evening hours, check those portions of your route that offered access to deeper water. Sink-tip lines become even more important in fall, because you'll be prospecting in deeper water, from five feet

Fall is a time for big flies because tiger muskies are looking for big meals.

to as deep as you're comfortable fishing with fly tackle. During the heat of the day, particularly when water temperatures may rise into the mid-fifties, you may have success by moving back into the shallows, which might have warmed enough to encourage tigers to forage there. Deep-water access nearby is important to tigers because temperatures there will be more stable. Edges, breaklines, and islands can all be productive.

This is a time for big flies, both because the forage fish are large by this time of the year and because the tigers are looking for big meals. As temperatures fall, slower retrieves will be in order.

Tackle and Gear for Tigers

Tackle for tigers has to do what tackle for northern pike must do, throw big flies. Rods designed to cast heavier lines will be needed. My recommendation to consider saltwater reels if you think you'll be traveling to the ocean to flyfish still stands.

Rods: I use nine- and ten-weight, nine- to ten-foot graphite rods for my tiger fishing, for the same reasons I use them for pike: they can efficiently throw the large, heavy flies that tigers prefer.

Reels: Again, I use the same reels that I use in my pike fishing. Because tigers hang in deeper cover during the summer, returning to the shallows to feed when the water cools in the morning and evening, the ability to change lines easily is important. If cost were an issue, I'd favor purchasing a less expensive reel if it meant that I could also buy a spare spool or two.

Lines: I fish for tigers using four basic line systems: floating lines with floating flies, floating lines with sinking flies, sink-tip lines with sinking flies, and sink-tip lines with floating flies. I use these combinations not only to place the fly where the fish are but also as a way of varying my presentation. In the case of sink-tip lines matched to floating flies, it's a way to prospect a fairly large column or "slice" of water.

A diver, matched to a sink-tip line, can work a five- or even six-foot column of water. A Bunny Fly, matched to a floating line, can zip just above the weeds in shallow water. Combine the Bunny Fly with a sink-tip line, and you can work deeper water or kick up mud in the shallows, making the fly appear to be a fleeing crayfish or baitfish.

All of these options become important at various times. Once again, I strongly recommend buying the best line you can afford. Because tigers love cover, the line is likely to take a beating from brush and weeds, and one of the new pike lines may be a good option to consider.

Leaders: As is the case with pike, you have two leader choices: composite wire/monofilament or straight mono setups, the latter option usually using hard monofilament for all or part of the leader.

There are pluses and minuses with each. Wire, because it's smaller in diameter, can cut through weed growth better than monofilament does. And wire is as close to being pike-proof as you can get. But even the plastic-coated, braided-wire formulations can kink, wire is more visible to fish, and knots can be a pain. Struggling to keep your Bic lit long enough to make a melt knot can sometimes be maddening.

Hard-monofilament shock tippets are larger in diameter than wire and can hang up in the weeds. Tigers have been known to bite through even hard-monofilament leaders, particularly when anglers forget to check the condition of the leader after each fish by passing the tippet between their lips to check for nicks.

I'd recommend fishing some of each and making a decision based on what you like to use. In my own case, I use level, twenty-five to thirty-pound hard-monofilament leaders for ninety percent of my pike and tiger fishing, and most of my leaders are between nine and twelve feet long, except in the fall of the year. At that time, when the fish spend more time in deep water, a long leader can slow the sink rate of your fly, and I use leaders three to perhaps six feet long.

As I mentioned in the chapter on northerns, Climax recently introduced a leader material made from a woven tungsten and steel formulation. This thin, supple, terrifically strong material promises to be the leader of choice for tigers as well as northerns.

Flies: Since I've caught most of my tigers on subsurface flies, they're what I tend to use most of the time: Both the D's Minnow and Strip Minnow patterns can be tied to produce very realistic impressions of baitfish and are durable enough to make them suitable for use with tigers.

For those who wish to fish a fly that's simpler to tie, the old standby Bunny Fly can be quite effective, particularly in white, black, and natural shades of brown and gray. For anglers starting out with lighter gear, the Barr 'Bou Face is a very effective substitute.

I also use a variety of divers in black, white, and "baitfish" gray, brown, or natural deer hair, highlighted with the discrete use of Krystal Flash, Flashabou, or tinsel. For tigers, I often fish divers as subsurface flies. This involves using divers in conjunction with sinking or sink-tip lines. The fly is cast and the line is permitted to sink. Then,

With all their peculiarities and challenges, tiger muskies are fabulous quarry for the flyrodder.

when the fly is retrieved, it dives much deeper than it would with float-ing line. I pause for a moment to permit the "cripple" to rise a bit and then strip again. Strikes often come on the rise, when the diver seems most vulnerable and your line is most slack. Be prepared!

There are also times to use floating flies. In Colorado, mid-June through mid-August marks the time when tigers seem most willing to accept surface presentations. The strikes can be terrifically violent. Divers, fished conventionally, are a fine choice, as are deer-hair or foam poppers and sliders. My tigers seem to like flies tied in a combination of black and purple. In the largemouth chapter, I mentioned fishing Bunny Flies dry. Tigers also love this presentation, perhaps thinking the fly is a furry creature of one sort or another.

Tigers, with all their peculiarities and challenges, are fabulous quarry for the flyrodder. By being patient and systematic and by spend-ing time on the water, you will catch tigers. This can be a mixed bless-ing, for with success, you're likely to become as fanatic about tiger hunting as I am.

NINE

GUILTY PLEASURES

I see that you're a flyfisher. It's easy to tell: one of your arms is three inches longer than the other and you keep making unconscious hauling movements with your shorter arm. Your graceful, stealthy gait tells me that you've waded silently and carefully for trout, across stream bottoms that would test the agility of a high wire artist. I see by your squinting eyes and sunburned nose that you've spent long hours peering against the glare from the water, trying to spot fish.

Yes, you've been some places, done some things, and caught some fish. And now, you're of a mind to seek out new challenges, new fish, new places where you can be alone with your thoughts and the whisper of your line.

This chapter is about such challenges, such fish, and such places. I will speak to you of the challenge of pursuing a fish that can touch your fly and count the wraps on the body before it spits it out. I will speak to you of a fish that, all the world over, is renowned as one of the great tackle-busting freshwater brawlers. I will speak to you of sticky, muddy bottoms, of undercut banks, of flooded brush, and of other places where lesser flyfishers fear to tread.

In this chapter, I will speak to you of carp.

All right, settle down! Stop whistling and booing. You can stamp your feet and shout all you want to, but this chapter is *still* about carp.

It just so happens that everywhere in the world, except in the United States, the carp is regarded as a terrific sport fish and as a fair table fish, as well—even the roe is edible and is often sold as a variety of caviar. Specific breeds, known generically as king carp, have been developed for cold water, for rapid growth, and (I'm not kidding) for the angler.

Go ahead, sneer. But while you do so, let me suggest to you that carp are perhaps the last great untapped flyfishing resource left in the United States, and that as a sport fish, it has smarts and raw physical power in abundance. American anglers have been missing out on one terrific fish, but hopefully, this chapter will convince you to give them a try.

My first experience with carp on a fly rod came about on a very slow day at a local reservoir. My friends and I were there to throw large

The last great untapped flyfishing resource, carp are a terrifically powerful fish that grows to a very respectable size. Brad Befus

flies at pike, but they'd moved into their summer mode and had begun to leave their spawning grounds for deeper water. We decided to check an inlet area, thinking that the cooler water there might have encouraged some pike to hang around.

We arrived during a damselfly emergence and the brush along the shore was literally covered with newly emerged damsels. Pike we had not, but we did see roiling water and, from time to time, the tips of large, forked tails. Carp had come into the shallows to feast on the damselfly nymphs. All in all, the situation was very reminiscent of bonefishing. Well, any fish is better than no fish, so we moved over to where the carp were working.

After tying on an olive Woolly Bugger, I cast to the closest concentration of tails, and one of them moved over to my fly. Cautiously, I raised my rod tip, and the instant I felt some resistance, I set the hook.

What happened next was quite interesting: the carp I'd hooked left for points unknown—smoothly and powerfully. The fact that I had the drag cranked down as tightly as I dared and that I was feathering the spool gingerly made not one bit of difference to the carp. (Bear in mind that I had come to fish for pike; I was using nine-weight tackle.)

I tried persuading the carp to stay, but I met with no success. It continued leaving. It continued leaving as it took the balance of my line. It continued leaving as it took the backing. And it continued leaving with my fly in its rubbery lip, leaving me with a slack line and an equally slack jaw. My friends gaped, too, and in very short order, they were casting Woolly Buggers and damselfly nymphs right beside me.

Those carp left, too—smoothly and powerfully.

We lost a bunch of Woolly Buggers that day. We did a lot more gaping, too. And we also landed a few carp in the eight- to twelve-pound class. We hooked, but never caught, some that were much larger.

Carp, as we learned that day, are a terrifically powerful fish and a fish that grows to very respectable sizes. The largest carp caught in the United States weighed almost fifty-eight pounds, and the largest carp caught on fly tackle weighed nearly thirty pounds. Carp are also very smart fish—with a life span of over twenty years in the wild and nearly a half-century when kept in ponds, they have plenty of time to learn a trick or two—and at times they are a reasonably catchable fish.

Doubling Your Pleasure

In this chapter, I'll be discussing two kinds of carp, the common carp, which was the carp we found tailing for nymphs and is a fish that

A perfectly legal immigrant, the common carp is known for its "subterminal" mouth and charming barbels.

you've probably met from time to time, and the grass carp or white amur, a fish that may be new to you.

The common carp (*Cyprinus carpio*) isn't native to North America. Originally found in Asia, carp have been *deliberately* stocked the world over. Whether or not you think it should have been, the carp was a perfectly legal immigrant to our shores, inasmuch as it made its way to the country under the auspices of the United States Fish Commission in 1876 when 345 adults were obtained and placed in breeding ponds. Since carp lay 150,000 eggs per pound of body weight, the Fish Commission was up to its bureaucratic ears in carp in very short order.

And how, you ask, did Old Bugle Lips subsequently make its way to virtually every lake, pond, and puddle in the land of the free and the home of the brave? By request! That's right, people would contact their congressmen and ask for carp. In the finest traditions of government boondogglery, carp were shipped all over the United States in special refrigerated railroad cars.

Remember that this all occurred over a century ago; our lakes and streams teemed with native fish. The fact that people wanted carp should give you some idea of the esteem in which the carp was held (or perhaps, of the questionable taste and judgment of our ancestors).

At any rate, centuries before anyone ever thought of catfish farms or trout farms, carp were being raised in ponds all over Europe and Asia, and I suppose our ancestors wanted to set up their own little carp farms, just like they had back in the old country.

Well, our great granddads succeeded beyond their wildest dreams, or perhaps beyond today's anglers' wildest nightmares. Clever carp soon managed to escape from the farm ponds into which they had been introduced, and their progeny now live everywhere.

This has provided fisheries managers with an ongoing headache, and in the interest of controlling carp populations, carp are one of the few fish that local regulations often permit and encourage being taken by any means available: rod and reel, nets, gaff, scuba spear fishing, bow and arrow, and tactical thermonuclear devices.

The second kind of carp is commonly called the grass carp. More properly it's a white amur, suffering under the Latin moniker *Cteno-pharyngodon idella*. Like the carp, it's a fish you may have met before, but you were likely carrying a nine-iron instead of a nine-weight. Beginning in the early 1960s, grass carp were imported from their native China to be stocked in golf course ponds and all kinds of other ponds and lakes that have weed growth that needs to be controlled. Stocking a few grass carp in a weed-choked farm pond can open it up in short order. The intent may be to provide a more pleasing appearance or better fishing for bass and sunfish already in the ponds, but those of us who have caught one know the real benefit of stocking grass carp is having grass carp to fish for.

Grass carp are members of the carp family, but their part of that family left the main trunk of the carp tree early on, and there are clear differences between grass carp and the common carp. Most important of these is that grass carp are largely vegetarian, preferring to eat plant life with only occasional insects and baitfish thrown in. It's that trait that has made them popular in this country. It helps that they're not successful spawners in lakes; they require large rivers to reproduce. This makes it very easy to control their population within a pond or lake and means that there's very little chance that grass carp will spread the way common carp have.

Grass carp are distinguished from common carp by three physical traits. First, they lack the spiny rays that common carp have on their dorsal and anal fins. Second, grass carp have a "terminal" mouth, meaning their mouth is on the front of their heads where most of us think a fish's mouth should be. Common carp definitely have "subterminal"

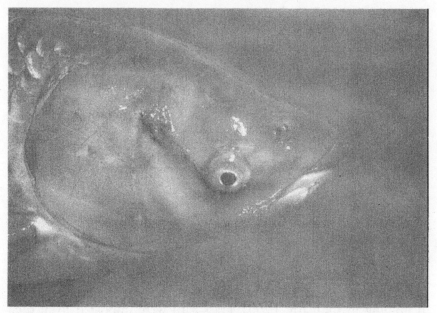

White amur or grass carp have a "terminal" mouth and no barbels. Except for the scales, you might not recognize them as members of the carp family. Brad Befus

mouths. Finally, grass carp lack the charming barbels extending from the mouth of the common carp. Except for the scales, you might not even recognize that white amur are members of the carp family.

Grass carp grow big. The world's record was a sixty-two pound fish caught in Alabama in 1991. This puts them in the king salmon category—and their raw power in the fight justifies that classification—but I've nicknamed them the Colorado tarpon. They've earned that title for their fantastic leaping ability. Common carp jump, but grass carp are acrobatic champions.

Like all shallow-water fish, grass carp are very spooky, and a stealthy approach and lots of patience are musts for the grass carp flyfisher. The aspiring grass carp angler must be willing to put up with numerous refusals and must be willing to stalk fish. But when a grass carp inhales the fly and puts its terrific strength to work, the flyfisher will be more than amply rewarded.

I also suspect that both kinds of carp, but grass carp in particular, are very intelligent. On a recent outing, I saw surface activity near a flower-covered bank. I carefully moved closer and watched in amazement as a grass carp grabbed a piece of floating brush and pulled it out of the way so it could approach the bank more closely and pluck flowers off the bank. Not exactly rocket science, I guess, but I've never seen a bass or trout perform as complex a task.

Carp Habits and Habitat

The carp is actually the largest member of the family that we anglers call minnows. Close relatives include the goldfish (with which the carp can interbreed), shiners, chubs, and daces. Lookalikes to which the carp is not related include the suckers. Since grass carp are relatively new and little is known about them from the angler's standpoint, I'll be discussing mainly the common carp in this section. Much of the information, however, applies to both species.

As you might guess, the common carp is a tremendously adaptable fish, and that adaptability makes zeroing in on carp difficult. In the previous chapters of this book, I've based much of the information about various species on the water temperature ranges they prefer. I will now do the same for carp: carp can live at ninety-six degrees for at least twenty-four hours. They can also tolerate literally being frozen for brief periods. Broad enough temperature window for you?

Let's try to narrow things down a bit more by discussing the water quality carp require. Carp can tolerate clear waters, turbid waters, oxygen-rich waters, and in impoundments that become oxygen-poor at certain times of the year, they can even survive by gulping oxygen directly from the air. That helps a lot, doesn't it?

Perhaps a discussion of the carp's preferred food will assist us. Common carp are, as everyone knows, usually bottom feeders. Carp can often be found working shallow bottoms, dredging along in search of their favorite food. And their favorite food is . . . everything.

Unlike the fish we've been discussing in preceding chapters, most carp are true omnivores, and they'll eat both plant and animal food happily. Insects, crustaceans, worms, other fish, fish eggs, and even carrion are part of the animal life they eat. Aquatic plants, flooded terrestrial vegetation, and even seeds make up the rest of their diet. In Colorado, for example, cottonwood trees distribute their seeds via a wind-borne cottony tuft that often lands on the surface of the water. Both kinds of carp will take these seeds from the surface, rising as consistently as trout to a mayfly hatch.

I've also seen common carp rise to such diverse snacks as dandelion seeds (eaten), potato chips (eaten), cigarette butts (rejected), orange peels (sometimes eaten), the remains of a bologna sandwich (eaten), aluminum foil (rejected), the remains from a can of worms (eaten, along with the bedding), a Hostess Twinkie that fell in the bottom of the boat and was tossed overboard (not just eaten, but fought over), fish entrails and skin (eaten—along with the heads, which somehow managed to make it down the carp's rather small mouths), and drifting insects of every kind.

This all sounds great, but it should be tempered by the following: unlike most of the fish I've been discussing, a carp doesn't make a rapid lunge for prey and wind up with a fly in its gullet. Rather, it extends its protractile, tube-shaped lips and mouths its meals. Their lips are very sensitive, and through them, carp obtain an immediate sense of what a prospective food item feels like. Something that doesn't feel like food is rejected—fast.

Secondly and again unlike most of the species we've been discussing, carp seem to have a well developed sense of taste or smell (or both). Laboratory tests have shown that carp have a definite preference for sweets. Bait anglers have known for years that garlic, cinnamon, and vanilla can all attract carp (that Twinkie must have been a very appealing snack). A fly that doesn't taste like food is rejected very, very quickly.

With this information in hand, we can now precisely define and summarize the carp's preferred living circumstances. Carp can live damn near anywhere. They can eat damn near anything. They can be active from when the water is so damn cold that it is barely liquid up to temperatures that are so damn warm that every other fish in the lake will either be dead or hiding in the depths.

Damn carp.

When I say carp can live everywhere, I mean everywhere. Many years ago, during a lunch break on a job site where I was working, I munched my sandwich beside an ornamental pond in the midst of an office park. I stared idly at the water and noticed that something was rising. They were grass carp. As I've said, white amur are more finicky eaters than common carp, adhering to a mainly vegetarian diet. They can grow very large, and they are very strong. Well, there weren't any signs saying that I couldn't fish, and I happened to have a fly rod in the car. In my fly box were a couple of white Woolly Buggers that looked a bit like the cottonwood seeds that the grass carp were slurping off of the surface.

I have no idea what the folks in the offices surrounding the pond thought about a flyfisher catching fifteen-pound fish from their ornamental pond. Unfortunately, the maintenance person who interrupted me made his thoughts on the matter quite clear.

Whether it comes from an ornamental pond or a farm pond, the acrobatic white amur is hard to beat as a sport fish, especially when it weighs over twenty pounds.

Strategies for Carp

As far as I know, no one, myself included, can call himself or herself an expert carp flyfisher. A few folks do it (and their numbers are growing each year) with varying amounts of success, and the general guidelines that follow are really a reflection of many experiments conducted by a number of anglers. There's plenty of room for more research on carp, especially on tactics that the flyfisher can use effectively. Perhaps you'll do some of it. Flyfishing for grass carp is practically an open field.

You've already heard me comment about flyfishing in an appropriate depth window, so I won't belabor the point here. What I will suggest is that there are times when carp can be found in shallow water, and that at those times, there are tactics that may work well for you.

But before I start that discussion, a warning or two is in order. Temperatures have been a focal point of this book thus far. I've used them as a means for determining where fish might be located and what they might be doing. It was such a simple system that it had to fall apart at some point, and with carp, I'm afraid that it does just that. As we've seen, carp can be active over a very wide temperature range.

I've also used the seasons of the fish (pre-spawn, spawn, and post-spawn) as signposts to further delineate what fish are doing at particular times of the year. Because of the carp's tremendous adaptability, this system likewise begins to break down. Carp can probably spawn within a wide range of temperatures—perhaps as low as fifty to as high as seventy degrees. With this sort of temperature window available to them, at any given moment you may be casting to pre-spawn, spawning, and post-spawn carp.

Carp are predominantly bottom feeders, but there are bottoms and there are bottoms. An ideal feeding ground offers both plant and animal food for cruising carp. As a general rule, weed growth and muddy bottoms that support abundant insect life are preferred. But fish don't live over twenty years by being stupid, so carp will also seek ready access to cover. Look for areas of very thick vegetation, undercut banks, snags, and downed timber. This kind of cover becomes a critical concern to the flyfisher, because unless you're using heavy gear, you're unlikely to stop a fifteen-pound carp when it dashes for cover and tries to wrap you up in the lily pads.

Carp will inspect your offering carefully if they can. But when groups of carp are actively feeding they stir up large clouds of mud. This gives you an excellent opportunity to present a carp with a fly while it's actively feeding and to present it when the carp needs to make a rapid decision, lest it lose the goody to one of its colleagues.

Like bonefish, a group of actively feeding carp cover the bottom quickly. When they're foraging in shallow water, floating lines and long leaders will do the job. But when the fish are deeper, short leaders, sink-tip lines, and weighted flies will permit you to fire your fly into the path of a cruising carp and get it on the bottom quickly, where it can be inhaled. This is important, for the following reason.

Predator fish catch their prey, and when we retrieve a fly, we're usually trying to persuade a fish like a northern or bass to chase down our fly and eat it. A carp, more or less, just happens across its food. Rarely does it have to chase anything. Although a strip or a twitch is always in order to bring your offering to the attention of a carp, I think you'll find that a real retrieve is wasted on it. The name of the game is putting your fly right in front of a feeding carp so that it can scoop it up along with the other plants and animals it's sucking off of the bottom.

Seasons of the Carp

Although seasonal changes and spawning times don't affect carp as much as they do other fish, an overview will help in your initial understanding of flyfishing for carp.

Pre-spawn Carp

Carp will become active in the kinds of fertile shallow areas that I described above almost immediately after ice-out, while the water temperature is still in the forties. Smaller carp will show up first, but as a rule they'll be sluggish until the water warms into the fifties. At this point active feeding begins, and you should start watching for "muds," areas of discolored water that indicate carp are feeding. Cast into those areas when you see them.

Spawning Carp

The pre-spawn season moves rather seamlessly into the spawn and post-spawn seasons because of the wide temperature range that spawning carp can tolerate. At any rate, as water temperatures rise into the sixties, spawning activities, characterized by much splashing, begin. The weedy shallows you fished earlier in the season for pre-spawn northern pike are ideal places to check for spawning carp.

At this time, carp are both less spooky and less interested in food than they are at other times of the year, but since post-spawn fish are also likely to be present, a cast to a muddy area is always in order.

Fly selection becomes interesting. Since carp will eat nearly everything, nearly everything has the potential to be at least inspected by them. Carp have small mouths compared to predator fish of the same

weight, and this will help you with fly selection. Rarely do I fish anything over about two inches long.

Some rudimentary hatch-matching may also be in order. Scoop up
some of the mud bottom and take a look at what you find therein. You
probably have something in your box that is at least of the same general
size. Remember that we're talking about a fish that will eat a small crawdad, a piece of drifting aquatic weed, or a sodden potato chip with equal
enthusiasm. A size 4 or 6 hook, palmered with a rabbit strip to give it
some action, can work well. Depending on its color, it might be taken
for a bit of weed dislodged by the rooting carp, a piece of decaying fish
flesh, a crumb of bread, or a sinking dandelion or cottonwood seed.

Post-spawn Carp

After spawning activities have concluded, you're likely to run into
carp that behave two ways. The first will be groups of carp that are
actively swimming, in a rather businesslike way, to some unknown des-
tination. I don't know what these fish are doing, but I do know what
they aren't doing—they aren't actively "dredging" for food. I treat
these carp like cruising bonefish, leading the school with my fly. Even
if it's not productive, it's good practice for the Bahamas.

The other behavior you'll see is active feeding. Some of the carp
will be in the shallows, going on about their business in typical carp
fashion: rooting around on the bottom, stirring up mud, and if the
water is shallow enough, tailing in the same way that feeding bonefish
do. I cast into the mud and try to trail along with the fish as they work
their way along the bottom.

At this time of year, water levels in reservoirs can be high, and you
may also find carp working very aggressively in flooded meadows and
brush. The first time this happened to me, I was fishing in a large reservoir in Missouri. The state had had record spring rains and the reservoir
was thirty feet higher than usual. I was fishing for bass, and although
the action wasn't exactly heart stopping, I was pulling largemouth out
from the flooded scrub with enough regularity to keep me at the task.

But even farther back in the flooded brush, there was an incredible amount of splashing and commotion, so much so that I thought it
might be an animal of some sort. Finally, I spotted carp that were rooting in the weeds, eating flooded spring plant growth and insects with
equal abandon. I weaseled my boat back into the brush and lobbed
some dragonfly nymphs at these fish. I had repeated hookups, followed
by short, thrilling runs, but the cover was so thick that the carp broke

The common carp, one of the most adaptable fish, is not just a bottom feeder. Carp flyfishers in the know carry "seed flies" for dry-fly action.

off almost immediately. I think I hooked five fish before I ran out of nymphs. I know I never landed any of them.

The second time it happened, I was fishing a small Colorado lake that is home to a good population of tiger muskies. It was spring and the water was high, flooding a grassy area that in the summer would be dry land. There was a commotion in the flooded pasture, and a group of spincasters were working the roiling water with big pike plugs.

I caught a glimpse of a tail and realized that the fish were white amur, happily grazing on grass and weeds. I moved over to the area, and threw my best "veggie fly" (a heavily-hackled olive Woolly Bugger) in front of the next tail I saw. I had terrific sport that day, catching perhaps ten grass carp that averaged twelve pounds each. Better still, when the spincasters saw that I was catching "trash" fish, they left, and I had the entire area to myself.

On occasion, you may be confronted with carp that are, if not rising, at least feeding on the surface. Probably, you'll see large groups of rubbery mouths gaping through the surface of the water. Often, this is accompanied by rather rude sucking, slurping noises as the carp work their way across the surface. These fish are worth casting to. Often they're sieving or slurping or sucking (whatever flyfishers will end up calling it) midges off the surface, and for these fish, Griffith's Gnats and other midge patterns work well. At other times, the carp are eating seeds, such as cottonwood, dandelion, or milkweed seeds. For these fish, a "seed fly" (a small, light hook palmered with white or cream hackle) will often induce a strike.

Bear in mind that these fish are feeding in a somewhat atypical manner and are therefore very cautious, in my experience. Your fly should be presented with all the delicacy you would use for skittish trout. Because carp feed in groups, you can often obtain a general sense of where surface-feeding carp are headed. Cast in front of the fish and let them happen across your fly. When you need to pick up your line to cast again, wait until the school has passed. It takes very little commotion to drive these fish back down to the bottom, and stealth is required.

My first experience with "seed flies" came about by accident. At the close of a day of pike fishing, I stopped at a local lake for a moment to cast to tigers. Tigers there were not, but carp there were, gliding around just under the surface, slurping cottonwood seeds from the film. I searched through every pocket in my vest for something smaller than the giant pike flies I was carrying that day. Finally, in the recesses of an inner pocket, I found a lonely, bedraggled, black stonefly nymph. In desperation, I cast the thing a few times, but it wasn't doing the job. The carp were in the mood for a salad bar, not meat and potatoes. What I needed was a way to imitate a cottonwood seed.

Perhaps necessity really is the mother of invention. Using my clippers, I trimmed all the material off of the stonefly, leaving a bare hook. Then, I clipped the white tail off a Bunny Fly and threaded it on the hook, much as a baitcaster would thread a worm. This, I decided, was a cottonwood seed fly. The carp agreed, taking the fly regularly, and giving me some fine end-of-the-day action.

Flyfishing for carp isn't something I set out to do—but it is something I will do if a good opportunity presents itself. My editor has the same approach to carp fishing. When he visited a Maryland farm pond in search of bass, he happened to notice large fish surfacing among grass clippings that had blown into the water when the farmer mowed around the pond. The fish were too large to be bass but were definitely interesting to him.

He asked the farmer what the fish were. Three-dollar-a-piece grass carp, he said, put in to control weed growth. The farmer invited him to fish for them because he wanted to know if the fish were good to eat.

Two things occurred to him immediately. One was that these big fish had been stocked only for utilitarian purposes; nobody was fishing for them even though they were nearly twice the length and probably four times the weight of the biggest bass in the pond. The second thing was a question: what was he going to use to imitate grass? "Matching the thatch," as he called it, was not something he'd ever had to do.

Like any good flyfisher, he was resourceful. He found a small green popper with rubber legs and cast it out in front of the rising amur. He didn't give it any action, figuring that grass didn't move that much. It wasn't long before the popper was slurped under, and a twenty-minute fight was on.

The white amur measured over twenty-two inches and weighed over six pounds. It had been stocked as a six-inch fish two years before. According to him, the grass carp fought as well as any fish he'd caught. Baked, it also made a very good dinner. So, why, he wondered, wasn't anyone fishing for the grass carp?

I think I may know why: frustration. I guess I'm one of the few flyfishers who are willing to be frustrated. I've even started fishing intentionally for grass carp, while common carp remain a secondary fish for me. Let me tell you how frustrating it can be.

Since grass carp don't usually move onto shallow flats until early afternoon, I spent the morning of a recent grass carp fishing trip chasing smallmouth. Finally I began to see tails and areas of roiling water. The time had come.

My partner and I quickly switched to Clouser Swimming Nymphs, and I began sneaking up on a solo fish that was rooting around about fifty yards up the bank. When I got to within sixty feet of the fish, I couldn't stand it anymore and I cast, placing the fly about two feet in

Frustration might be the thing that keeps more flyfishers from fishing for white amur. Smart and strong, there are many ways to lose a grass carp. Brad Befus

front of the tailing grass carp. The fish turned toward the fly and quietly made it disappear. It started to move off; I lifted the rod slowly until I felt the weight of the fish and set the hook, hard.

There was a great splash, and the fish simply disappeared. I still had it though. My line was cutting through the water, and the fish was clearly making a run toward a tree that had fallen into the water. I had two options. I could apply pressure and try to turn the fish, but trying to hold a twenty-pound grass carp with 3x tippet didn't appeal to me. Option two was to let the fish run and wait to see what would happen. I chose option two and waited for the inevitable foul up in the deadfall. Did the grass carp run under the tree? No. It jumped the tree, Colorado-tarpon style. Grass carp continue to amaze me.

One disaster was averted, and we settled into a tug of war that lasted twenty minutes. By leaning on the rod, side to side, I was finally able to wear the fish down, but as usual, frustration was just ahead. As I attempted to land it, the grass carp snapped my tippet in one final surge of power. I hooked three grass carp that day, all probably over twenty pounds. I don't know for sure, because I never landed one of those smart, strong, damn fish. Frustration.

Tackle and Gear for Carp

Although it's unlikely you'll rush out to purchase new equipment for carp fishing, I thought I should make some general recommendations in case you have more than one outfit in the car.

Rods: Since I don't usually set out to fish for carp, most of my carp fishing is done with whatever tackle I happen to be using at the time. I've hooked carp on four-weight trout rods and light trout leaders. While lots of fun, this usually doesn't last very long. When I do fish for carp intentionally, I use anything from a seven- to a nine-weight rod.

Reels: Once again, I most often use what I have, but when I do some serious flyfishing for carp, I use my saltwater reel. Unlike virtually all of the fish I've been discussing, carp will spool you. No kidding. If you've been looking for an excuse to buy a saltwater-grade reel with a better drag and more backing capacity than is generally offered in freshwater reels, carp provide ample justification. The ability to change spools quickly and easily in order to take advantage of surface and subsurface feeders is also important.

Lines: Floating lines will handle the bulk of your carp fishing, but I would recommend always having a sink-tip line (which you probably already have, right?) close at hand.

Leaders: There's room for experimentation here. I think, but I cannot prove, that carp can be quite leader shy and that this is particularly true of surface-feeding carp. One approach is to use light leaders, but carp are strong. Landing a carp on a delicate trout leader will require finesse and no small amount of luck.

I suspect that this may be a place where the new fluoropolymer leaders (Spiderwire and the like), which are very strong in relation to their diameter, may be used profitably.

Flies: Over the past few years, some friends and I have tinkered with a variety of patterns for shallow-water carp. Most notably, Brad Befus' spin-off of a bonefish fly, aptly named Agent Orange, has accounted for good numbers of large carp in shallow water. This fly is presented in the color plate section.

One of my favorite times to fish for carp is when some of our local lakes experience dense damselfly hatches, and at this time a variety of damselfly nymph and adult imitations work well, as does an olive Woolly Bugger. In addition to these offerings, I would also recommend having a seed fly, like the one I described earlier. Scuds, particularly in orange, and midge pupas and dries are also good flies to have at hand. I'll leave it up to you to decide how to "match the thatch" for grass carp.

Carp are smart, big, and strong, but flyfishing for them is a relatively new idea, and prejudice about the fish keeps anglers, particularly flyfishers, from fishing for them. Much remains to be learned and overcome. On a slow day when not much is happening but I see an area of roily, shallow water or during a dead calm summer day when my canoe is suddenly surrounded by a field of gaping mouths, I'll take the opportunity to cast to carp. I recommend you approach common carp with the same kind of attitude. (I think you may decide that fishing for white amur is another matter—you may end up intentionally fishing for them as I do.)

Misgivings and prejudice will be quickly replaced with respect once you've wrestled with one of these fish. However you approach it, I can assure you that if you end up with twenty pounds of carp or white amur on the end of your line, you'll be suitably impressed.

INDEX